FUNDAMENTALS

Surfing

FUNDAMENTALS

NAT YOUNG

THE BODY PRESS
A division of
PRICE STERN SLOAN, INC.

©1985 by Nat Young
Published by The Body Press
A division of Price Stern Sloan, Inc.
360 North La Cienga Boulevard
Los Angeles, California 90048

Printed in Singapore by
Huntsmen Offset Printing, Pte, Ltd.

Design by John Witzig and Tony Gordon
Photography by Peter Simons and Tony Nolan

Library of Congress Cataloging-in-Publication Data

Young, Nat, 1947-
    Surfing fundamentals / Nat Young.
        p.   cm.
    ISBN 0-89586-688-9 (pbk.): $10.95
    1. Surfing.   I. Title.
GV840.S8Y69   1988   87-23065
797.3'3—dc19   CIP

CONTENTS

INTRODUCTION

IN the first part of this book I have detailed the basics of surfing. My knowledge was gained through thirty years of experience and my understanding of how to teach the fundamentals to both kids and adults through a program I wrote and instigated for the first surf school in Australia.

The book begins with some good exercises and the difference between swimming in the ocean and swimming in fresh water. It then takes you step by step through the motions of learning to ride the ocean's waves on a surfboard from standing up to turning on the face. Part 2 is informed surfing and deals with advanced manoeuvres, competitive surfing and surfing big waves, as well as a few chapters that will be of interest to more involved surfers.

Because surfing is not just board-riding, I have covered body surfing, the Boogie board and the art of riding a Malibu board. In recent years many surfers have turned to riding wave skis and for this reason I have had the experienced Phil Avalon write the chapter on wave ski surfing. As did Australian champion kneelo David Parkes write on kneeboarding.

The other day I was surfing one of my favourite haunts (the Wedge at Whale Beach). After a couple of good clean driving lefts I managed to scratch into one a little bit bigger. The bottom turn was intense. As I relaxed the pressure out of the turn, my concentration was distracted by another surfer coming down on the same wave. For a second our eyes met and we recognised one another. My fear of being on an 8' wave with someone who couldn't surf was discarded and I was off to the top of the wave. In inimitable style, Tommy Carrol was about to blast a full on bottom turn. The next time our tracks crossed, we had time to say 'G'day'. We were now in the flow of the same energy. On our next high speed pass we just smiled and kept our respective feet flat to the floor for the inside section, confident in each others ability to ride the wave without causing an accident. It was like Tom was on lead and I was on base, the wave creating the rhythm. To competent surfers the similarity between surfing and music is obvious but this type of surfing is for experienced surfers only as is surfing big waves and advance manoeuvres like aerials.

Whatever standard you are up to in surfing the book can be used as a reference. Treat the ocean with respect and good surfing.

Nat Young

PART 1
BASIC SURFING

1   No wave will simply pick you up. You must learn to paddle a surfboard before anything else is even attempted.

2   Never allow the surfboard to drift sideways (i.e. parallel to the shoreline and the incoming waves). Always have it pointed straight in or straight out.

3   Every manoeuvre in surfing requires balance and momentum. Think back to the first steps in learning to ride a bicycle, and the importance of getting a good push-off. Surfing is no different.

4   To catch a wave you must paddle at the speed of the moving swell.

Starting out right

Doing it just right!
Crouched low – arms
outstretched – eyes on
the section ahead.

SURFING ability is a combination of several different skills. Naturally the beginning surfer must be a competent swimmer, but he must also be able to paddle and handle his surfboard with confidence in the surf before concerning himself with the balance and co-ordination required to stand up and ride a wave. The basic manoeuvres are standardised, it is their expression that sets surfers apart, and makes the difference between good and bad surfing. There are a number of ways of telling that difference but the one I use constantly is to watch the nose of the board. If it remains close to the water surface throughout all manoeuvres and situations, the surfer is extracting the maximum from his board at all times.

SWIMMING

Before you surf you must learn to swim in the ocean, which is a very different place to a pool or river. How fast you swim is not important. What really matters is stamina. The novice should be able to swim a kilometre straight, and two kilometres with a short rest between. The basic difference in ocean swimming technique is that the head must be kept up at all times. The main reason for this is to avoid loose surfboards, bluebottles, seaweed, and any of the other hazards the ocean might throw up.

EXERCISES

A reserve of energy is vital if you are to deal with all situations in the ocean. Here are a few exercises that have helped me build and maintain a high energy level.

The first can be practised in a pool or even your bath – holding your breath under water. At first it feels like you will burst, but with practice you will find that you are capable of increasing the time you can stay under.

Sometimes the force of a wave can hold you down and without the abil-

13

ity to stay under water for at least 60 seconds, you can be drowned. My most unforgettable hold down was not as you would expect in Hawaii but at Dee Why Point in Sydney, where I rode my first waves over 3 metres. I was pinned to the bottom on the take-off and unable to move for the endless time it seemed to take for the next wave to pass over. The important thing to remember in this situation is to keep calm. Don't struggle, wait until the pressure subsides, then open your eyes and swim to the surface avoiding the bouts of white water. Take a breath and a quick look because you are in the impact zone, the place where the wave exerts maximum force when it breaks. Be prepared to dive again as soon as you have observed the circumstances.

As an exercise used to strengthen your legs and in particular your calf muscles there is a ski exercise that will seem impossible at first. With practise it will really strengthen the thighs and calf muscles. Standing with your back to a wall, feet 45 cm out from the base of the wall, sink down to a sitting position, hold for 15 seconds, or less if the pain is intolerable. Rest and then do it again. You should feel the muscles in your legs become tight. This exercise is of real benefit when you are surfing good waves and having more than one session a day.

Paddling practice is a good exercise. We go into this in some detail later but it is important to note here that the ability to paddle well can make the difference in staying safe in a big sea. Aside from this there are obvious benefits in being able to catch the waves you want. Paddling muscles take time to develop. You must allow at least a week of concentrated paddling before you are ready to seriously consider catching a wave. I have noticed, particularly with girls, that the hip bones become bruised and sore if too much is attempted too soon.

As a warm-up exercise a quick jog along the beach before hitting the surf is not a bad idea, or any other warm-up program to get the blood circulating and loosen the muscles.

SKATEBOARDING

Being a competent skateboard rider really helps. Many of today's pros started out turning in a carpark or playground. Skateboard-riding is an excellent confidence booster. It's relatively easy and safe if done in the right area. The action of turning is similar in that you learn to hold down and release pressure with each manoeuvre and is lots of fun.

I have found that some kids are genuinely afraid of the ocean and waves in particular. Sometimes the fear can be attributed to over-zealous parents and other times to a nasty experience while just a crawler. In any case it's not a good idea to push children into the ocean.

BODY SURFING

Although you don't have to be a good body surfer to learn to ride a surfboard, the understanding of the ocean and timing gained from body surfing is a tremendous help to the novice boardrider. I would advise all surfers to learn the art of body surfing.

14

Above – *Skate boarding – the grommets' best training for surfing.*
Left – *Simple stretching exercises – even the pro's do it before every surf.*

One great advantage of body surfing is that you don't have to be concerned with equipment. The only thing you need is a flexible body and the ability to shape and control it on a wave. Riding a broken wave on the body can give good understanding of this body movement. Choose a sandbank with waves breaking outside and rolling across the bank in about knee- to calf-deep water. Once in water of this depth let the first wave go; it will put more water over the bank for you to ride in. Watch the oncoming second wave carefully and turn your body towards the beach, still watching over your shoulder. Crouch as if you were going to jump, and, as the wave begins to lift you, spring forward into the foam. Take a deep breath and

stretch your arms forward, your hands together, one over the other, simulating the bow of a boat. This makes your entry as smooth as possible. Give a little kick with your feet if necessary; you'll find yourself gliding with the momentum of the wave towards the shore. Practise this a few times before tackling an unbroken wave. The method for doing this we describe next.

Swim out towards the waves and when the first wave is approximately one metre from you take a good breath and dive under it coming up after it has passed over you. Then swim back to the surface and continue in this way until you are beyond the breaking waves. The larger the wave the deeper you must dive. Once you are beyond the break, tread water. You'll find yourself rising up with the swells as they pass. When you see a wave that looks like it will break in the normal pattern, make up your mind to catch it. As the wave approaches, turn towards the beach, watch the wave over your shoulder and begin to swim with its crest. As you feel the power of the wave taking you with it, give one more stroke and let your arms move back alongside you. Pull them in nice and close, stick your chest out, lift your chin up, and by kicking your legs you should be able to stay with the wave. As the wave dissipates towards the beach you will find it necessary to kick more and perhaps further streamline your body by hunching your shoulders and concaving your chest. Taking another breath and burying your head will help you stay with the wave.

The first few times you decide to try and ride an unbroken wave you should choose your location carefully. Choose an area where a lifeguard is on duty. Should you get into any difficulty then he can offer assistance. Make sure the waves are not dumping. This is very important, as a wave that dumps is difficult to ride, especially in the area where it *does* dump after the lip has broken for the first time. A dumper is caused by a wave breaking on a shallow sandbank, generally at low tide, so what you must do is find a deep water sandbank. When the tide is high, the wave will tend to roll rather than dump or pound onto the sandbar.

You should soon be ready, in this type of surf, to go sideways along the wave like a surfboard rider. For 'cornering', as it's called, it is helpful to pull your leading arm out of the water, put it forward and use your shoulder and arm to adjust your position on the wave face.

Rubber fins (or flippers) can be used as an aid to body surfing. They increase the kicking area of your foot and give it flex, which enables you to propel yourself faster when catching the wave and when attempting to stay with its momentum. Fins come in four sizes to ensure a tight fit, but it is a good idea to tie a cord loosely around your ankles to be doubly sure you don't loose them. When entering the water, walk backwards or you'll find yourself flat on your face in the sand.

Bodysurfing – the purest form of surfing is great fun in the shore break and an important way to gain understanding of the ocean's power.

Choosing your Surfboard

ONCE you have made up your mind to learn to surf the first problem facing you is selecting the right surfboard.

The best type of surfboard for a beginner is the lightest, widest board you can find. And it must be thick. A good length for a learner is around 3 metres. You'll never ride it in the tube or on a hollow wave, but it will float you well, it'll be stable, easy to paddle and easy to stand on. You probably won't want to keep such a board once you've mastered the basics, but it will make the initial steps so much easier that I believe the extra expense involved is justified. Ideally you could borrow one, but even if you have to pay as much as $300, there are so few good learning boards around that you will be able to resell it for much the same price.

Before selecting a surfboard from a surfshop-rack ask the salesman's advice. He is there to help you and although it's only his opinion most employees in surf shops are experienced surfers. The advice costs you nothing. If you're buying from a newspaper advertisement it's best to take along someone who knows and understands surfboards. Have a good look at what is available before you buy.

Avoid radical looking surfboards or homemade 'backyard jobs'. Flotation is all important. You must buy a board that will float your weight.

The type of beginner's board I described earlier in this chapter is called a Modern Malibu but because they are hard to find second-hand you may have to settle for an older modern board. Choose one with a full plan shape and plenty of thickness.

The quality and condition of the surfboard you buy will depend on how much you are willing to spend on it. Don't waste your time on old, battered boards. They are often impossible to repair and are completely useless unless they *are* repaired. They let in water, which makes them heavy and ruins the bond between fibreglass and foam. Instead set yourself a figure within your budget, and remember that surfing equipment is relatively cheap because, after your initial outlay, you have very few expenses.

If a board is on its last legs many tell-tale signs show up. The foam turns yellow or brown, showing that it has been left exposed to water and sun for long periods. The fibreglass will eventually lift off the foam. If you can't see the foam be sceptical. Compare the weight with another surfboard the same size; if it is heavier the chances are that the colour is hiding something. Feel around the edges of the board and especially the deck to make sure there are no soft spots.

Make sure the fin is secure and look for cracks at the base where it joins the board. On the subject of how many fins the ideal beginner's board should have I have no hard and fast rules. The most important point is floatation so if you find a twin fin with all the right qualities to suit you con-

sider it. Certainly twin fins turn easier than singles but they do not have as much momentum. The same rule applies to tri fins or thrusters but naturally the risk of getting cut by having more fins is increased. For this reason alone I believe the ideal beginners board is a single fin.

BASIC ACCESSORIES

After you've bought your board you need minimal additional equipment. If you're a beginner you don't need a leg-rope. Leg-ropes do save swims but they can be dangerous, and there are a number of circumstances in which a beginner certainly should not be tied to his board. Quite a few injuries have been sustained through their use, and it would be wise to go through basic training without one. The only time I use a rope is when I'm surfing in front of rocks where a fall could result in a lot of damage to my board. If as a beginner, you feel you must use a rope then buy a good one and attach it properly. Don't secure it to the fin because, if the board pulls back suddenly, there is every chance of the surfer being struck by the fin. A fin attachment also creates drag, which makes the board travel slower. Attach the rope with a plug countersunk into the deck of the board. Most new boards have plugs built in but, if yours hasn't, you can make one. Make a loop out of strands of fibreglass, soak it in resin and drape it over a pencil or similar object on the deck near the tail.

There are many brands of leg ropes on the market, varying in price from $10 to $20. A padded ankle strap for comfort and double swivel make the cord tend not to tangle which is especially helpful if you are falling off a lot. If you don't use the board constantly, remember to wash out the swivel in fresh water as the brass will corrode. But give careful consideration to the pros and cons of wearing a leg-rope. As well as the obvious danger factor, there is the possibility that the novice will come to rely on the rope and not try to correct the bad points in his surfing technique. If every mistake means a swim to the beach, the beginner will soon learn to be a better surfer and swimmer.

If you learn in summer you will only need a pair of board-shorts. Again, there is a wide variety to choose from but the best shorts have two fixings: a clip and a drawcord, or a clip plus Velcro strip. The style of shorts is not important, but it's wise to remember that boardshorts often have to put up with a lot of strain, and anything less than good quality, well-stitched material will not last too long.

Some people start to learn to surf in winter or in year-round cold climates. I don't advise it as muscles tense up in cold air and water temperatures. It is necessary here to mention the wetsuit, something that can make all the difference in cold weather. With a wetsuit on you can spend longer in the

Choose your first board carefully – it must float your weight, have soft low rails, and preferably a single fin.

19

water and considerably speed up the learning process. Wetsuits are made of neoprene rubber with a nylon backing to give extra support. The amount of rubber you should have covering your body depends on how cold it is and how susceptible to cold you are. A vest is usually enough to keep off a cold breeze, but continual cold water surfing means more rubber; anything up to a full-length suit where only your face is exposed. A wet suit's warmth is created by the neoprene only being able to absorb a certain amount of water. This water is heated by direct contact with your body and you stay warm until the next time you dive under a wave. If you develop a rash around your neck or under your arms the first few times you wear your suit don't be particularly alarmed, take a big glob of vaseline and apply it to the sore area. After a couple of surfs the problem should be solved. Either that or the wetsuit is an incorrect fit and can be discarded. As much as possible endeavour to wash the suit in fresh water as this keeps the neoprene soft and stops the colour fading.

The final accessory you will need is wax. This is important because without it you will have a hard time lying on your board, let alone standing on it. Wax should be rubbed all over the top or deck of the board every time you go surfing.

You build up wax on your board by applying a coat each time you go surfing. It is important to apply the base coat or first coat 0.5 cm thick uniformly over the entire deck. Be sure to wax off and over the rails, but not on to the bottom, especially where you would hold the board while rolling under a wave (about one-third down the length of the board from the nose).

These days there are many surfboard waxes on the market. In the old days surfers used straight paraffin, but these days the recipes are closely kept secrets. Basically they are mixtures of paraffin, beeswax, and incense. The greater the content of beeswax the more sticky and softer the wax. This method is used in the making of cold-climate wax. The exotic smells are liquid incense and the colour is food dye.

On a new board, especially in a warm climate where you need harder wax, a good method of getting on your base coat is by melting it in boiling water. Get hold of an old jam tin and fill it with boiling water, lay it beside your board on the grass, take the bar of wax and dip it in the hot water for a few seconds, then pick it out and rub it on until it becomes difficult to rub on. Repeat this process until the board has an even cover.

Beginners usually develop a chest and stomach irritation from lying on the waxed surface. Also contact along the insides of the legs often causes a rash. This can be avoided by wearing a tee-shirt and applying calamine lotion as soon as the rash is first noticed.

In recent years we have identified the position on a thruster style board where we want to stand while riding a wave. As a substitute for wax, inventive surfers have developed a thin rubber pad that has an adhesive backing sheet. The trading names of these products differ around the world, in Australia the most popular one is Gorilla Grip, and in the USA as Astro Deck.

Right – Rub wax everywhere on the deck. Wax provides a sticky rough surface for paddling and standing on.

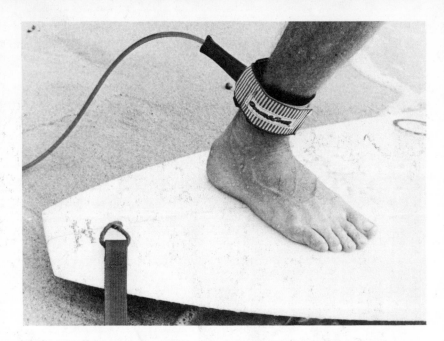

Above – Attach the cord to your back foot. Kids with small ankles should be sure to get an adjustable strap.

Learning to Paddle

THINK of your new board as a see-saw. You must lie a little behind centre in order to keep the nose out of the water and maintain balance. It's a good idea to practise in still water first, a lake or a pool will do, and in a short time you'll have lying on your board completely organised. But don't be misled; even in still water it's not as easy as it looks. If you take the time to practise in a pool you are less likely to be knocked off your board the first time a wave hits you.

Don't make the mistake of lying too far back on the board. Although it's easier to balance from this position, as soon as you try to paddle you'll be in trouble because the tail will be too far under water for fast movement. Keep the nose as close to the water as possible, or at most a couple of centimetres above the water level. Your positioning on the board is extremely important. You should lie with chest and shoulders raised so that the lower part of your rib cage is the first part of your body actually touching the deck. Although this is difficult to do at first, it doesn't take long to learn and the position allows for better breathing. If you lie flat on your chest you have to lift your entire torso a few centimetres each time you inhale, and this usually results in shorter breaths being taken. Keep your feet close together and remember that any part of you hanging in the water creates drag. On boards where your feet and part of your legs are in the water, counter the drag effect by keeping them together when you are paddling.

The arm motion for paddling is similar to the Australian crawl swimming action; each arm stroke alternately. It has been found by most surfers that short, shallow strokes are more effective than the deep strokes that beginners tend to use. There is no need to lift the arms right out of the water after each stroke. Simply keep your arms close to the board and let your strokes synchronise with the board's speed.

As the muscles become accustomed to paddling you will find it less strenuous. As your paddling improves simulate the wave-catching situation. Paddle hard in bursts of 30 seconds to a minute, then sit up and drop your legs over the side of the board. From the sitting position (actually it's a straddling position) try to turn the board in a complete circle. This is done by shifting your weight towards the tail and frog-kicking with your feet. Use your hands like a rudder to assist in the turn. Turning the board from this straddle position is something you should become skilful at, because you will need to turn fast to catch waves and to avoid side-on encounters with a breaking wave.

Another handy thing to practise in still water is launching the board. Stand at the edge of the pool or lake, hold the board with a hand on each edge (rail) and deck facing you. Imagine that a wave is approaching and, as it reaches you, leap over it and onto your board and start paddling with the momentum the leap has given you. This is the technique you will later employ when entering the water from rocks, and it can also be useful when pushing through the break.

During the 1960s, and in fact ever since surfboards have been ridden, the position for paddling them has been both prone and on your knees. With the advent of smaller boards – the average size of a normal performance board being just over two metres – it was impossible for the board to be paddled on the knees because it sank, the bulk weight being concentrated in one position. When lying prone, the weight is spread over the entire board and the board paddles easily. Completely disregard the knee-paddling technique. It is not practised on the smaller, modern surfboards.

The Power Glove is a revolutionary new product of the 80's. Basically it's a rubber glove that does for the hands what the webbed feet do for the duck. There are several different brand names available at your local surf shop for around $25.00. Some are more bulky than others, the latex rubber variety are thinner and lighter, however, you must take care when putting them on by using talcum powder. Also, moving around and over rocks could damage the glove. Some surfers' arm muscles take a little time to adjust to the extra water resistance but these products really add to your paddle power.

Right – *Paddling using alternate strokes keeping the nose just above the water.*

*Quality beachbreak like this is the perfect spot to begin
your surfing experience. Slow peeling waves breaking in
one well defined area.*

22

Into the Ocean

THE basic rule to remember once you have entered the ocean is this – keep a constant, observant eye on waves. They are sneaky things that you must learn to understand and use to your benefit. Before you hit the water, sit down on the beach and watch. Pretend you are paddling out, turning around, paddling again and catching a wave. Observe how the wave breaks and think of the situations you would have encountered if you'd actually caught it. If you have the patience (and to learn to surf you're going to need a lot of that) watch quite a few waves until you have some idea of their breaking pattern. The longer you spend watching the more comfortable you'll feel out there.

Choose your beginner's spot carefully; a break that rolls rather than pounds onto a sandbank. Some beach where the waves break a fair distance out and roll slowly to the beach. Choose a 'smallish' day and avoid a crowd, but make sure someone is about in case you get into any trouble.

It is a good idea to check the wave size by watching another surfer on a wave. If the waves are over his head it is advisable to wait for a smaller day. A rip or current of water flowing back to the sea in one corner of the break can be an advantage if it is not too strong. Experienced surfers use the rip as an elevator to the break but they can be dangerous for novices. Remember that the larger the waves the stronger the rip.

The ideal set-up for your first encounters is a gently sloping beach break with a slight rip in the lee of a headland. Here you will be able to paddle out easily without danger of being carried away from the break.

When you first go down to the shoreline carry your board under your arm. Don't drag it across the sand. If it won't fit under your arm (and a good, wide beginner's board may not) balance it on your head and use your hands to steady it.

At the water's edge hold the board in front of you as you did at the edge of the pool. If there is a high tide and a sloping shoreline, you'll be able to start straight off with a bit of momentum. Stand to the side of the board that feels the most comfortable and, as a wave rushes towards you, leap over it and onto your board, assuming the normal prone paddling position. The first few times you attempt this the fin may catch in the sand, so make sure there's about thirty centimetres of water under your board. The timing of your leap is most important.

Right – *Ex-world champion Mark Richards jumping over the shore break to help gain momentum for the paddle out.*

PADDLING OUT

If you have chosen a break which has a rip to one side, you will not have to paddle through broken waves. But of course you will have to learn how to do this eventually so it's as well to know the basic techniques for getting through them before you start. The easiest and most common method of meeting a broken wave if you are a beginner involves sitting astride the board.

As the wave approaches, slip to the back of the board and turn it from the sitting position 180° so that the nose faces the beach. Slip both hands just forward of your knees and hold the rails tight, then let the wave wash over you. You will lose considerable ground with this method but sometimes it can be effective. Your feet act as anchors and prevent you from going all the way to the beach with the wave.

Sometimes when the broken wave is small and not very powerful you put your hands flat on your board (while lying in the prone paddling position) about equal with your shoulders. As the wave approaches you rise up

Above – Impact zone – from the water it looks like this – waves break in shallower water, deeper water takes the energy back to sea.

Right – Try to avoid this situation by taking a good long look before you enter the water.

off the board as if you were doing a push-up and let the wave pass between you and the board. This saves any slowing-up contact with the wave and you should still have some momentum left to continue paddling, particularly if you've given a couple of hard strokes beforehand.

I should mention here that there is another method of encountering broken waves – if you happen to be wearing a leg-rope. On occasions surfers simply push their boards aside and dive for the bottom when confronted with a big wave about to dump on them. If you do use this method make sure there are no other surfers behind you or in the vicinity of where your board will be washed by the oncoming wave. This practise really should only be used in emergencies and good surfers are rarely caught out in this compromising position.

IMPACT ZONE

There is one place in a surfing area that a beginner should avoid at all times – the impact zone. The water pitched out by the falling crest of the wave is called the lip, and where it lands is the impact zone. The full energy of the wave is directed on this spot and for those few seconds it is an extremely dangerous place to be. The power of the lip is dependent upon the depth of water over the reef or sandbank on which the wave breaks. The direction and size of the swell also have a bearing on this but, as a general rule, stay clear of the impact zone. If you happen to be confronted with the lip while paddling out; either paddle faster to break through the wall or wave's face before it breaks or hang back and let the wave break a safe distance ahead of you. It's a matter of using good judgement, but if you can't avoid the lip then slide off your board as smoothly and quickly as possible and dive deep. Open your eyes underwater and when you can see that the turbulence has passed, swim to the surface, look out for the next wave and start swimming for shore.

Catching a Wave

NO wave is going to pick you up and give you a free ride. Sometimes a wave will burst upon you and punch the board forward, but nine times out of ten it will simply pass you by because you have not matched your paddling energy with the energy of the wave.

BROKEN WAVES

Paddle the board out towards the incoming waves and push through as many as you can. When you feel that at this stage of your progress you can go no further, push through one more for luck. Sit up and turn the board to face the beach. If at all possible try to have these first few encounters on the ideal location, where a sandbank has just enough water over it that without waves the water depth is somewhere between knees and hips. The advantage here is that you can slip off and either lift or turn the board around until it is facing the beach at right angles to the oncoming wave. Slide back onto your board and paddle towards the beach watching the approaching wave over your shoulder. At this point the wave's energy will replace yours, and you can lift your arms out of the water and grab the rails of the board with both hands. As this happens your feet will be higher than the rest of your body; to prevent the nose from digging in (pearling) you must shift your weight towards the tail of the board. In fact your board is a see-saw and the wave is its constantly-changing fulcrum.

For your first few rides go directly to shore in this position, getting off when the wave has deposited your board on the sand. Or, if the wave backs off in deeper water and reforms to dump on the sand, slide off the back and stay underwater until the board has come to rest on the sand and can't bounce back and hit you.

You could repeat this for hours, just to get used to the feel of the transfer of energy from you to the wave.

ANGLING OR CORNERING

The grip you have on the rails in this position is rather like holding handlebars. To corner, simply apply pressure, and lean in one direction as you are sliding down the wave. The board will respond and turn either right or left. Be careful not to apply too much pressure or lean too long, because the board will turn off the waves. Change your direction, then centre your balance again. Do this until you feel confident that you understand how a surfboard turns.

CATCHING AN UNBROKEN WAVE

This is the next step and an entirely new concept. Firstly, you must decide which wave you will catch, and this is where the time you spent watching the waves from the beach comes into play. If you've watched the pattern of the waves at the break you've chosen, you'll be in a much better position to choose a good wave. Remember that you are going to catch a real one. Not one that has already broken and expelled its energy, but a wave that could well have travelled a thousand kilometres as a swell to break right here and now just for you.

Waves generally come in sets of five to ten, but when they haven't travelled far (i.e. they have been generated by local winds) they are likely to be close together and uneven. Often they are just like large chop, particularly in summer on the eastern seaboards of Australia and America.

Once you have reached the area just beyond the breaking waves (the take-off area) find a reference point on the beach (a tree, a house or car) that will give you a constant idea of your position; in the ocean nothing stays in the same place for very long. When you are satisfied that you are in the best position for catching waves, sit up and wait for a set to approach. Single out the wave you want. Usually the second wave of a set is the best because you can coast on the swell of the first to be in perfect position for it. Paddle directly towards the beach as the wave approaches, making sure there are no obstacles in front of you, because now your concentration must be centred on catching the wave. Remember that to catch a wave your paddling speed must match the speed of the wave.

A good rule for catching your first waves is that when you think you're on the wave give one final stroke as the board slides down the face. Slip to the back to avoid pearling, grab the rails with both hands and direct the board where you want to go as you did when riding broken waves. When you have reached the bottom of the wave's face move back up the board slightly to put it into trim for the ride to the beach.

Some experienced surfers might feel that the learning techniques I have suggested in this chapter are somewhat humiliating for the beginner. I would point out once again that the ocean is extremely unpredictable, and one of the best ways I know of learning about a surf break is to ride a few in the prone position. I have acquainted myself with some of the best breaks in the world – like Lennox Head and Rincon – by catching my first wave in that prone low-centre-of-gravity position. I do this because it gives me insight into the peculiarities of the wave's formation. I can see without having to concentrate, all I do is hold on to the rails and glide around the wave, looking at where the curl breaks without running the risk of being knocked off. Every wave in a session will not be exactly the same but if it's a point or reef-breaking wave on a constant bottom shape, and providing the swell is consistent, the waves will be similar enough.

Right – *Paddle for the wave as hard as you can – when you think you have it, give one more stroke.*

Standing up

WHEN you are absolutely sure you have caught the wave, and you've given that one last stroke, keep the board flat on the water. Make sure it's not inclined towards either rail, and keep your weight centred as you prepare to stand up. Place both your hands flat on the deck directly below your shoulders as you would to do a push-up. Press your weight up high enough to bring one leg up and under your chin and let the other leg follow behind. Land on the balls of your feet and stand flat-footed, your front foot down the board and your back foot across it.

If you spend some time practising this movement on the living room floor, and then do it with your board placed on a soft surface, you should be reasonably adept by the time you attempt it on a wave. Take care that you land on the right spot in the centre of the board or slightly towards the tail, where the board can continue to travel down the wave face. If you stand too close to the tail, the nose will lift out of the water and force the board off the back of the wave. If you stand too far forward, you will force the nose under the water and nose dive or pearl.

Don't be afraid to spread your feet wide apart. About shoulder-width apart is ideal but do whatever feels comfortable. The idea is that you can control the pitch of the board with your feet and correct a roll to either side by leaning in the opposite direction. You may find that it helps to stretch out your arms like a tight-rope walker for extra balance.

There are two different ways to stand on a surfboard, and most surfers have a preference for one and use it almost exclusively. A 'natural foot' stands with his left foot forward. A 'goofy foot' stands with his right foot forward. Which foot you put forward does not matter. Again it's simply a matter of whichever feels most comfortable, like which hand you write with.

A natural foot faces the wave when he rides right (i.e. right to left as you watch from the beach), and has his back to it when he rides left. The situation is reversed for a goofy foot. Riding facing the wave is called 'forehand', and riding with your back to it 'backhand'. You will probably find it easier to surf forehand initially as you can keep your eye on the wave, but backhand surfing is equally important and should be practised whenever possible.

Most surfers employ a slightly different stance for surfing backhand. Both feet are placed across the board with the heels close to the inside rail (i.e. the rail closest to the wave face), but this is a technique that seems to come naturally and should present no problem for the beginner.

Learning to stand steadily on a surfboard takes quite a bit of practice. Don't immediately try to change the board's direction, just ride straight to the beach. And don't be discouraged by the number of times you fall off.

But remember to surface with your hand above your head after every fall. Only once have I seen a surfer pop his head out of the water to meet his board coming down, but the accident was near fatal. Also, keep a lookout for the next wave. There could be another loose board in it, and a crack from behind can be very painful.

The most common mistake in learning to stand up is not keeping your knees bent, at least enough to absorb the bumps in the wave. Remember that any sudden movement in you produces an even more sudden movement in the board. Be as fluid as possible.

Once you've mastered standing up you'll probably be tempted to move forward on the board. This is fine on a rolling wave, but on unbroken steeper waves you would be better advised to step or lean back until you ride out the drop, this being the most critical part of the unbroken wave when it initially breaks. When you've survived the drop then step or lean forward to stay on the wave.

It is important here to mention the art of falling off, because you will no doubt be doing plenty of that. Although you cannot always control where you fall, you should try as much as possible to fall into the face or white water of the wave, where the board will not be, as it is running ahead of the wave towards the beach. Try not to fall off the other side because there you run the risk of being hit by your board as the wave washes it to shore.

The time to turn your attention to travelling sideways along the wave is when you have mastered the basics of standing up and making it to the beach without falling off. If you've followed the instructions in this chapter on catching a wave you will have already angled the board from the prone position and you can do exactly the same standing up by simply pointing the board in that direction as you get to your feet. The principle is the same. You must keep the board on a line.

Right – Draw your hands out of the water and place them close to your chest. Press up, until your arms are fully extended, using knees and toes swing your body underneath your arms. Land flat-footed, stance as wide as possible, knees bent to absorb the shock, arms spread out to maintain balance.

Basic Manoeuvres in Modern Surfing

THE TAKE-OFF. This is the name given to the starting point on a wave. The take-off is made when the wave is peaking or reaching its greatest height before breaking. Because the wave is at such a critical point there is small margin for error. In many cases a successful take-off results in a good ride, while a poor take-off can ruin positioning for the whole ride.

It's worthwhile mentioning that you can get off to a good start for an angled ride by paddling with your board pointed slightly in the direction you want to travel. This will all but eliminate the need to turn once you are standing up.

The normal method of taking off is to paddle directly towards the shore at a 90 degree angle from the line of the wave. This will place you in perfect position for a bottom turn. Expert surfers can take off at almost any angle, either facing away from the curl or facing towards it, but beginners should stick to the simple 90 degree angle take-offs. There is also a method of taking off paddling into the curl, which has advantages when the wave is moving slowly and you want to gain extra acceleration for your bottom turn. This is for competent surfers only.

FIRST TURN

As you become more competent you will learn to change your position on the wave to either avoid the curl or increase your speed. Positioning is all important, and the best way to change position on the wave is to turn the board. Turning either increases or decreases the speed of the board, and I consider it to be the most important manoeuvre.

The turn is not a throwing movement. The surfer does not move to the bottom of the wave and throw his body and board away from the impact zone, although beginners often find that this is the automatic reaction. Instead, the action should be more like the recoiling of a spring. As you arrive at the base of a wave an effective turn is made by bending the knees as low as they can go and releasing the spring by rising up slowly and leaning in the direction you want the board to turn.

THE FLICK OFF OR KICK OUT

As the name implies this is a method of getting off the wave. As you travel across a wave you may decide that the section of wave in front of you is impossible to beat, or there may be rocks or other surfers in the way. So you have to get off the wave.

The standard 'pull out' is achieved by moving to the back of the board, lifting the nose out of the water and leaning in the direction you want the board to travel. To make this movement quicker, jerk the board up the wave face or, if you can make the weight change smooth and controlled, the board will leave the wave cleanly.

Right – *Back hand take-off – difficult because you can't see where the wave will break.*

Left top – *First turn – taking off in the direction you want to go. At the bottom of the wave, lean over, bending the knees, pushing gently.*

Left bottom – *Flick out – when the wave closes out your bottom turn is extended up through the lip and over the back of the wave.*

*Dropping in – the surfer on the inside, closest to the curl
has the right to the wave. Crowded conditions are difficult,
try to understand the other surfer's position, communicate.*

Helpful Hints

WITH a growing number of surfers hunting and riding the same number of waves it is essential that the beginner has some understanding of the unwritten rules of surfing.

When a surfer is up and riding a wave he has the undisputed right of way. It is the job of the other surfers to avoid any collision and to stay out of his line because the only thing he can be concerned with is riding that wave. Accidents often occur when a surfer or surfers paddling out try to make it over the shoulder or unbroken face of a wave being ridden by another surfer. This is an extremely dangerous practice. If you are paddling out it is better to roll through the white water than to interfere with someone else's wave. The surfer on the wave is heading for the shoulder. Everyone else should head somewhere different.

When two or more surfers paddle for the same wave the rule is that the surfer on the inside (i.e. closest to the curl) has the right of way. But there are variations on this general rule. If you are surfing a peak break with other surfers and one begins to paddle for a wave, ask which way he or she intends to go. If you can go the other way without interfering at the take-off then do so. But if the other surfer doesn't answer, it is wise to let the wave go. Your time will come.

As a beginner you are obliged to be respectful of another surfer's superior ability. Always yield prior to a situation of conflict. There are only a certain number of waves in a set, and there are never enough good waves to satisfy even good surfers. The better surfer will always get the better wave, the same as the better fisherman, the fish. Before you can ride a good wave you have to learn to ride on bad waves.

This 'code' may seem a little unfair. But you must remember that a good wave cannot be ridden well by an inexperienced surfer. To become a good surfer years of dedicated practice are necessary. Once you are a good surfer you will appreciate the need for some 'code' if you are to surf at all.

On the north coast there is a good surf beach called Angourie, with almost the perfect surfboard wave on the right swell. Not so many years ago the place was isolated. You had to walk along a sandy path where there were three fishing shacks nestled in the lee of a grassy headland. The emus and kangaroos (big reddish brown ones) would look up startled by the sight of man in their area, then bound away down the track. Later on the track became a road and years later the road was sealed. At that time surfers were already settling in the area. Good surfers living there now with families and friends, know how to surf Angourie, know every rock, every change the wave makes as it moves around the point and on to the rock shelf. It's their home, and like thousands of surfers around the world, the local surf break is an important part of their environment. My point is, respect and courtesy are due in a situation like this.

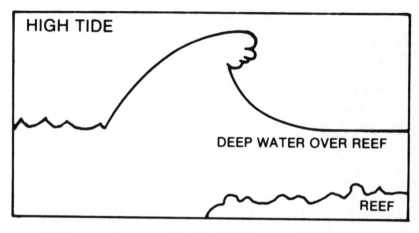

HIGH TIDE

DEEP WATER OVER REEF

REEF

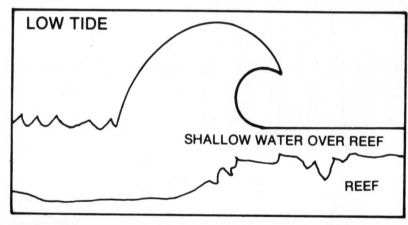

LOW TIDE

SHALLOW WATER OVER REEF

REEF

Waves break more at low tide, because the water is shallower.

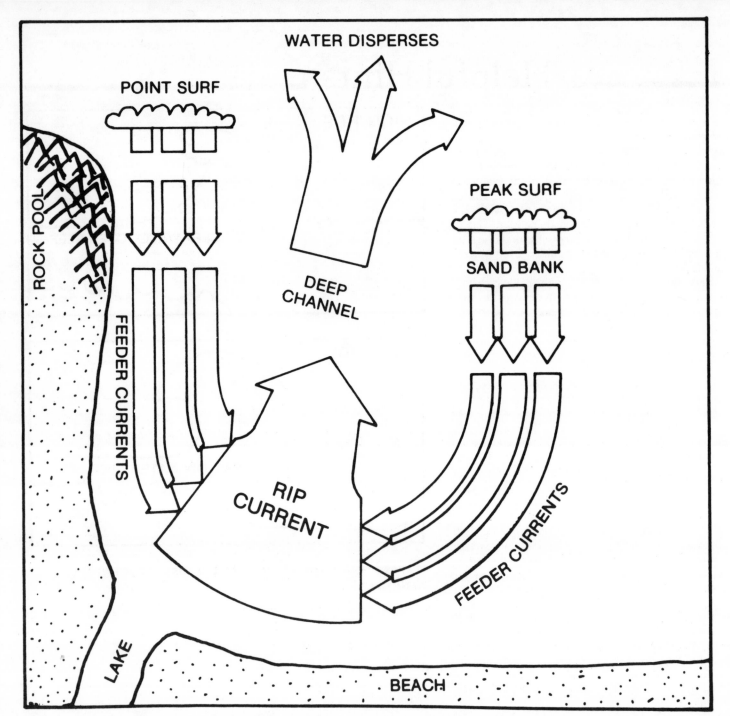

WATER DISPERSES

POINT SURF

PEAK SURF

SAND BANK

DEEP CHANNEL

ROCK POOL

FEEDER CURRENTS

FEEDER CURRENTS

RIP CURRENT

LAKE

BEACH

This setup at North Narrabeen is typical of what occurs in the corner of beaches everywhere.

I learned my lesson the hard way. When I was surfing every day there weren't the crowds, and still I hassled other surfers for wave priority, and created a bad vibe. I was finally taught a hard lesson in Hawaii, where the Hawaiians command respect from surfers who come to ride their islands' waves.

RIPS

These are the channels between breaks, the place where the water which comes in with the waves flows back out to sea. Surfers often use slow moving rips to paddle back out to the break, but fast moving rips are best avoided. Should you be caught in a rip without your board don't panic. Swim across to the nearest break and stay in the white water until you are washed to the beach. Most rips have maximum power between breaks. Further out to sea they are less powerful and easier to swim away from. If you can't, use the common distress signal – one arm raised above your head.

Below – *Injured fellow surfer – everyone lends assistance.*

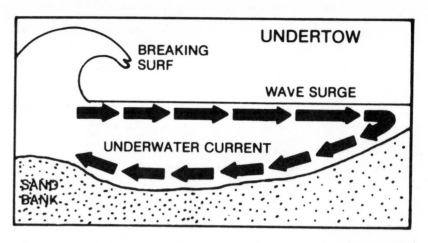

Above – *Undertows – take a good deep breath and go with the current – you will come up.*

Above – *Wipe out in the lip, usually the worst way to go, it's a long way to the bottom and you run the risk of hitting the board.*

Right – *Wipe out in the bottom. Don't fight it, go with the waves' power, stay under water till the pressure has subsided.*

WIPE-OUTS

Wiping outs or falling off can be dangerous, particularly in a big surf. We've already mentioned the basic method of avoiding a collision with your own board, but in bigger surf there are other aspects to consider. Try to fall away from the wave's impact zone, either into the face or off the front of the board ahead of the impact. On a sandbank it doesn't really matter whether you land feet or head first but over coral or a shallow reef try to land feet first and roll into a ball. This will help you roll with the turbulence and avoid head injury.

In big surf the golden rule is relax. Don't panic. Take a good, deep breath and dive with the lip, going deep enough to avoid the worst of the turbulence. Open your eyes and look for the patches of still water between the areas of turbulence and surge. Swim to the surface avoiding the turbulent patches, take another deep breath and look out for the next wave. Chances are you'll be right in the impact zone, and you'll have to dive deep again.

COLD WATER

A good, warm wetsuit is an absolute necessity. It's almost impossible to surf when you're cold and your muscles are stiff. As we've noted earlier, design and thickness of rubber should be determined by personal need with regard to how cold it gets where you intend to surf. Neoprene Booties are another accessory that is essential in cold water surfing. Be sure to get them nice and tight as movement between the foot and the rubber will create obvious problems. When putting the bootie on roll it back and insert the toes, rolling it on over the foot and up the ankle. As well as being excellent insulation against cold water booties serve as a real protective barrier when surfing over rocks and coral reefs.

Below – The most exciting waves for good surfers are disastrous for beginners.

WARM WATER

This is much more exacting. You become tired very quickly. Take it easy, make sure your skin is protected from too much sun, and remember that warm water breeds marine life that can bite and sting. Coral cuts are a real problem in the tropics so be sure to treat every cut with the potential to becoming ulcerated. Wash in antiseptic and apply anti-biotic ointment.

ROCKS

It is a good idea for beginners to stay right away from them. You'll occasionally see surfers taking off close to rocks and narrowly missing them. Rest assured that these surfers know the break well. If you do fall off in shallow water over rocks, let the white water wash over the shelf, unless it is going to deposit you on bare rock, in which case you should swim as hard as you can against the pull of the wave. If you can't break through it then wrap your arms around your head, curl into a ball and try to land feet first.

LOOKING AFTER YOURSELF

In hot weather sunburn can be a hazard, especially for beginners. The sun reflects off the water and exposes surfers to high levels of ultra-violet radiation which causes burning. Fair skinned people in particular are affected and intense sunburn can land you in hospital. The nose and lips are usually the most susceptible and even the best available products, zinc and UV creams, come off after a period in the water.

The eyes and ears are quite vulnerable to salt water exposure, and if you surf a lot you are in for problems in both areas. The ear is not equipped for constant immersion in cold water, and almost without exception every surfer who spends more than twenty years in the water will find it necessary to undergo an operation to remove the bone growing inwards in the ear canal. I use ear plugs whenever I surf, but some surfers claim this affects their balance.

Ear infections seem to thrive in warm water and special care should be taken in places like Bali and Hawaii. A careful wash and dry with cotton buds is a good idea after each surf.

After some years of salt water exposure pterygium are prone to form in the corner of surfer's eyes. These too can be removed quite simply. Irritation from sand or coral can be avoided by rinsing the eyes after surfing.

Cuts and abrasions require special care because constant soaking prevents the formation of a scab. Small cuts often develop into ulcers. Try to limit your surfing time until the wound heals. It'll pay off in the long run because the time you'll spend sitting on the beach nursing an ulcer will be a lot longer.

CRAMP

Cramps occur mostly in cold water as a result of overexposure or going in the water too soon after a meal. You should wait at least half an hour after eating any food. At the first sign of cramp head back to the beach and massage the affected area. Stretching the muscles also helps.

MOUTH TO MOUTH RESUSCITATION

All surfers should at least know the basic procedure involved in preventing a drowning. Tilt the patient's head back as far as possible to open an air passage. Keep the neck fully extended and the passage open. Take a deep breath, open your mouth wide and place it over the patient's, sealing off his nostrils with your cheek. Breathe into the patient's mouth; forcefully for an adult, gently for a child. Take your mouth away and watch for the patient's chest to rise, indicating that he has started to breathe again. Listen for the sound of air escaping from his lungs. The process should be repeated until both these indications have been noticed. The first few breaths you apply should be in quick succession, then at a normal rate – ten to fifteen breaths a minute. Maintain this until a doctor arrives.

Above – *Rocky shelves are not the place for the inexperienced.*

Caring for your Surfboard

LIKE many other modern toys, the surfboard is not very durable. It is built for performance and how long it lasts is largely up to you. As most first surfboards are purchased collectively by parents for gifts and kids who have worked hard to go surfing it is important to mention the correct method of looking after your new board. Whatever its condition it's your new board and from the moment you walk out of the surf shop it's your responsibility.

Actually from the time you lift the board from the rack and walk with it to the counter disaster can strike. First, if the board won't fit under your arm, carry it on your head, fin down in order not to hit anyone or anything. Never stand the board up against a flat wall or the counter of the shop, inevitably it will fall over. Instead lay it flat on the floor or on its edge if space is tight. The same rules apply when you get the board home. Many a ding has happened on the first night in the bedroom of the new owner with all the best of intentions.

The next morning when you go to tie the board on the car's rack take care not to pull the expandable straps or ropes too tight. Remember surfboards are made of foam and fibreglass, not steel or wood, so too much pressure and you can pull right through the rail.

When you arrive at the beach and lay your board down to wax it, look out for anything sharp in the sand or grass. Little rocks can penetrate the single layer of fibreglass on the bottom as soon as you apply pressure on the deck. Also take care not to expose the waxed deck to intense sunshine as the wax will melt within a minute or two.

One minor point about leg ropes. If yours doesn't have a swivel at each end I don't suggest you wrap it around the fins as many experienced surfers do – it will tend to tangle easily. Whatever you do, either attaching it to the roof rack, or tucking it in the board cover, be sure not to drag the velcro ankle strap on the ground while walking to the water's edge. It will pick up grass and sand and will eventually clog up.

The decision on whether or not to put the board in a cover depends on the quality of the board. A canvas or towelling cover keeps off the sun's ultraviolet rays which tend to turn the foam a brown colour. A cover also helps keep wax off the bottom that seems to get there no matter how much care you take. A quick wipe over the running surface with a towel before you surf is a good habit to develop. Cloth covers give very little protection against dings, however travel covers that are padded with plastic bubbles in between two layers of nylon are a good development.

The quality of materials used in surfboard construction is extremely important. I suggest you buy only from well-known, reputable manufacturers. Others may be using poor quality foam or resin which will break down easily.

Right – *Four channel thruster – the most popular design in the eighties.*

Above – *Necessary equipment for repairing your board.*

Left – *Board covers help protect your board from scratches and wax.*

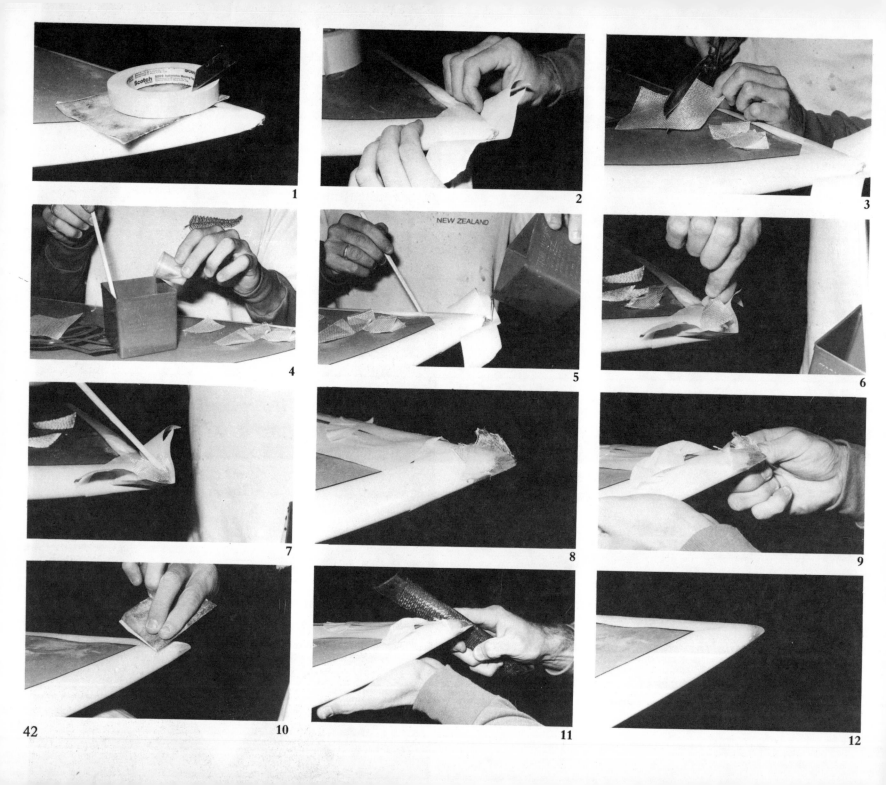

These days a lot of boards are sold on the strength of the designer's name. There are quite a few top surfers who shape and design excellent boards, but it's as well to consider how much of the design is functional and how much is fashionable. Will that shiny triple-fanger wing tail be a fading memory this time next year? By choosing a simple and functional design you can maximise the board's resale value while a dozen new fads come and go.

Surfboards are made from a polyurethane foam core or 'blank', covered with resin-saturated fibreglass. The foam blank is poured in a mould and then a stringer of thin wood is glued down the centre to give lateral strength. The shaper then carves his design from the blank with a power planer and a variety of sanding equipment. The board is then 'glassed'. Fibreglass cloth is draped over one side at a time and saturated with laminating resin – a special type of resin that hardens slowly with the addition of a catalyst or 'hardener'. Glassing is a job for experts only. A little too much catalyst and the board becomes very brittle. After the fin is secured with fibreglass rope (more about that later) another coat of filler resin is applied. Then the board is sanded using electrical sanders and a final coat of finishing resin applied. One more sanding using wet and dry paper, a polish, and the board is complete. Surfboard production is improving all the time. There is still room for improvement in materials. For a long time now surfers have been trying to reduce the weight of the foam blank. Perhaps technology will come up with a core substance that combines with air, like honeycomb.

FIXING DINGS

Experience will tell you when a ding needs immediate attention before you use the board again, and when there is no need to repair, but here are a few things to look for.

If the board is knocked slightly a white pattern of fibreglass will often appear on the surface. This is known as a 'shatter' and there is no need to have it repaired. The fibreglass skin has not been penetrated and the board is not taking in water. Dents in the surface don't warrant attention either, unless they are on the running surface and are big enough to affect the board's performance, in which case they should be filled and sanded back to the contour of the board. Dings that do penetrate the skin should be fixed immediately because if water gets in, the foam will discolour and the fibreglass will lift away from it.

Left – Steps in the repairing process of the common nose snub. Taped up and ready; cutting fibreglass; mixing resin and catalyst; applying fibreglass to give strength; using stirring stick to saturate cloth; cutting away excess with razor-blade; sanding with surform; fine sanding with glass paper; ready for finish coat.

STEP 1: Make sure there is no water in the ding. Hair dryers are good for quick drying or, if you have plenty of time, leave it in the sun for an hour or two. Clean away the splintered fibreglass with a knife or razor blade and rough up the area to be bonded using coarse sandpaper. Fibreglass won't bond on a smooth surface.

STEP 2: If the ding is small it can be filled with chopped fibreglass or glass bubbles, a powder that thickens resin. For bigger dings (like the common leg-rope cut) I advise shaping a piece of foam to fit the area. Glue it in with resin, let it dry, then shape it to fit the contour of the board. Remember to shape it slightly smaller to allow for the fibreglass cover.

STEP 3: Mix up your resin and catalyst. The proportions you should use are listed on all repair kits, or if you've simply bought the materials from a surfboard factory, ask someone there. Usually the mixing proportions are two or three drops of hardener to a small jar of resin, but this varies with the temperature, so it is not a good idea to do your repairs in the sunlight. Make sure the mix is properly stirred.

STEP 4: If you're patching a small ding rub styrene (liquid resin thinner) into the weave of the fibreglass before you start. This will make it almost invisible when finished. Build up the area with layers of resin-saturated fibreglass until it's above the surface of the board. Ten minutes after the resin has begun to gel take a Surform blade and sand the area down to its pre-ding shape. Fine-sand it with sandpaper, remove the scratches with wet and dry paper, rub a touch of toothpaste into it for a final cut and polish, and the board should be as good as new.

REPLACING THE FIN

This is a common repair that can be quite costly unless you do it yourself. An electric sander is the best tool for the job. The fin should be replaced or reset when the base cracks to such an extent that the fin is no longer stable in the water. You'll feel the board go rubbery and wobble through your manoeuvres.

STEP 1: If the base is simply cracked, take a sander, use it delicately with a new, coarse disc and cut away the built-up resin between the bottom of the board and the fin, until you can remove the fin. Clean up both the fin and the base area.

STEP 2: If the old fin has fallen out in the water you'll have to buy a new one. Don't try to make your own. Getting the right amount of rigidity and flex is a job for experts.

Pencil mark the approximate centre of the fin. Mix up a small amount of resin and catalyst and pour onto the base area. Sit the fin in the resin. Here it is essential to have a friend at hand to check from various angles that the fin is sitting perpendicular to the board. When you are both sure that it is, tape it in place from the tip to the outer edges of the board.

STEP 3: Now you will need fibreglass rope or rovings. When you buy ask for enough to replace a fin. Divide this in two equal parts and lay out on a piece of cardboard so that resin can soak into the strands. Cut pieces of fibreglass cloth the length of the base and wide enough to lap over onto the bottom of the board and up the fin.

STEP 4: Mix up another batch of resin and catalyst. You'll need about 140 ml of laminating resin and about 10 ml of catalyst to ensure a slow mix, and the slower the mix the stronger the job. Paint the base of the fin with resin and pour a small amount over the rovings on the cardboard, making sure they are saturated. Use a squeegee or piece of cardboard to remove excess resin and lay the rovings along either side of the base. Work it in with your fingers. Place two pieces of fibreglass cloth on top of the rovings on each side and hold them in place until the mix starts to go off. Then filler coat the whole area, with particular attention to the area at the front and back of the fin. While the mix is still gelling, sand it back to match the contour of the board, using a Surform. If you have an electric sander use it to sand the area once the mix has gone hard. Finish the job with either a finish coat or wet and dry sandpaper and a polish. If you have left a bead of resin around the edge of the fin after finish-coating, be sure to sand it away because it will cause the fin to hum. If the fin is new and hasn't been foiled let an expert do it for best results. The front edge should be blunt, the back sharp, but not sharp enough to cut. Fin foil is much like the cross-section of an aeroplane wing.

Below – Broken boards happen rarely but are a fact of life with modern light equipment.

Things that Bite and Sting

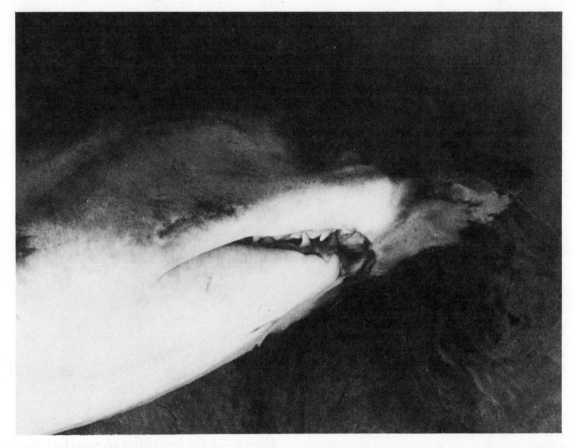

Every surfer has to come to terms with the possibility of shark attack.

THE ocean is a totally new environment for the novice surfer and in most cases he or she knows little about the creatures who live there. Some basic information is vital.

Very few sea creatures are vicious. Even the shark has been misunderstood. But they do have seasonal habits of which you should be aware.

SHARKS

I believe the shark has been the victim, particularly in Australia, of a highly dramatised campaign of discredit. I've never seen one while I've been surfing. However they are out there, and I suppose surfers and divers have more to fear from shark attack than do people who spend less time in the ocean. There are few preventative measures you can take if a shark decides to attack. But if you are always alert and if, in the case of an attack, you actually see the shark, your chances of avoiding injury are fairly even. On the few occasions that I have been led to believe there was a shark near the break, closer examination has revealed it to be either a dolphin or a sunfish, both of which are harmless fellow surfers. The old belief that sharks don't go where there are dolphins is not true and in fact, in the day time, sharks and dolphins are usually in the same area. The dolphin on the surface and the shark some 10 metres below in order to pick up the left overs. By night the dolphin sleeps in a colony with their eyes closed and sentries posted. If

a cruising shark who sleeps with eyes open while swimming should come upon a colony of sleeping dolphins the guards will attack immediately.

Many city beaches are meshed to deter sharks, but it seems they favour areas near river estuaries or where effluent is disposed of. Late evenings are said to be the most likey times of attack. Statistics from Manly Marineland over the past eighty years show that most attacks happen between 3 and 9 pm with a quarter past five being the worst time. Skin divers have a lot more to fear from sharks, but to me it seems only natural that the hunter should expect to sometimes be the hunted.

Sharks are apparently endowed with sophisticated radar systems that pick up signals from other animals a mile away. They have been known to swim past 100 people to get to the one who has urinated – this being one

Above – *A fin breaking the surface is a terrifying experience. Mostly it's dolphins or sunfish.*

Right – *Bluebottle – scourge of summer surfing the east coast of Australia.*

Far right – *Sea urchins – nestle in rocks and crannies of rock and coral all over the world.*

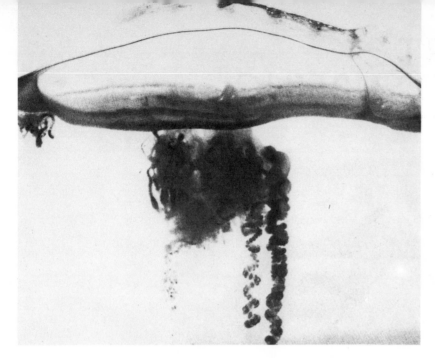

of the first indications of an animal in distress. They can detect signs of human panic immediately, so the vibe you have in the water is important. If you're terrified of shark attack, a shark in the area will probably sense it.

SEA SNAKES

These nasty little creatures (usually 30 to 60 cm long) have a highly venomous bite but they are not aggressive. They live in the warm waters of the tropics, notably Bali and Hawaii. Australian surfer Bruce Raymond was attacked in Hawaii a couple of years ago. A bite can be fatal within minutes and there is no antidote. The fangs are set well back in the mouth and the sea snake's bite is confined to a narrow area.

THE FISHDOCTOR

These are more of a joke than a threat, but they do bite with their long nippers. A kind of miniature crab, the fishdoctor goes for the hairy part of the body. Irritable but not dangerous.

BLUEBOTTLES

Common in Australia, these are easily recognised by their blue air sacs, which float on or near the surface. The sac acts as a sail while the sting is confined to the long tail which dangles below like a thread of blue cotton. The longer ones will wrap around your body several times unless you are careful. The thing to do is keep a cool head despite the pain of being stung. Reach down and remove the tentacle from your skin without breaking it. Get to the beach as quickly as possible, apply fresh water and an antibiotic spray. Don't rub the sting with wet sand because this will cause it to spread and get into the pores of your skin.

JELLYFISH

These are ususally blue, brown or translucent. Most of them sting, some worse than others. They can be picked up by the jelly, but avoid the tentacles which contain the sting. Generally their sting is not as painful as the bluebottle's but it should be treated in the same fashion. Beware of particularly bright coloured jellyfish; some varieties usually found in the tropics are deadly.

FRESHWATER LICE

Lice most often appear with jellyfish and seaweed or after heavy rain. They invade the surf at river and lake entrances and cause itchy little bumps like mosquito bites. They can be painful, particularly if large numbers of them bite you in the more vulnerable areas of your body.

SEA URCHINS

These are balls of spines generally 5 to 10 cm in diameter. They live in rock crevices on the waterline and are often found at reef and point breaks. Surfers often tread on them and find that the spines can be painful and hard to remove from the feet. They have a tendency to break off, but it is essential that the whole spine be removed to avoid infection. When you are entering or leaving the surf over rocks you should always tread carefully and not in crevices between the rocks.

PART 2
INFORMED SURFING

1   Relax – go with the ocean's energy. You will never overpower the force of nature.

2   Never be caught flat footed, stiff and locked in to one position on the board. It is bound to end in a wipe-out.

3   Developing the ability to be able to turn into position is the key to modern surfing.

4   Every turn is a matter of breathing out while bending in the knees and breathing in to finish the turn.

Advanced Manoeuvres

THE surfboard has been refined tremendously over the years and we have defined the position from where we want the maximum speed. On a modern multi-fin board this point is right under your feet when you first stand up. On a Malibu it was necessary to move forward several feet to find the trim (see Malibu Chapter Section 3). In the 70's we had to move a few inches to find trim, now it is only a matter of a few centimetres. Newly developed products like the 'Rocket Block' and 'Action Traction' are available at surf shops. Placed in the correct position they further help define the fastest position on a multi-fin board.

Generally speaking, you should be standing right on the tail in waves under a metre and slightly forward in bigger waves. Minor adjustments are important. Sometimes you will see an experienced surfer bouncing the board up and down on a particularly slow section of wave face in order to get more speed – this action is effective because you are weighting and unweighting.

This brings us right into the most important ingredient in surfing a small modern surfboard.

TURNING AND BREATHING

If you will remember back to the chapter on Basic Surfing concerning your first turn, I talked about the action of a spring coiling and uncoiling in order to turn in the direction you wish to go. To expand on that theory it should be very easy to understand that the bending of the knees or recoiling of the spring is a breathing-out action.

The pushing of the board out of the turn is a breathing-in action associated with standing more upright to finish the turn. You will find this style of breathing comes perfectly naturally and most surfers don't even think about it until it's been brought to their attention. This process of split-second weighting and unweighting co-ordinated with your turns is the same as in skiing, and 90 per cent of all surfing turns are made like this. The

Below – *The bottom turn seen from any angle is a compression and extension associated with weighting and unweighting.*

knees bent to absorb the action. The body straightening to carve the arc. It is one of the subtleties that separate competent from good surfers and should be constantly practised. You can also turn a surfboard by pivoting it around right in the curl. This is a slowing down manoeuvre and can be executed without power. It is a helpful move in order to let the curl catch up.

Although turning sounds rather complicated it is actually very basic stuff, and after you've blown a hundred bottom turns and thought about what went wrong, you should begin to understand the theory. I have proven it to myself over and over again and I still occasionally make mistakes. Sometimes I might not hold the weight long enough and end up a metre away from where I want to be and get nailed by the collapsing curl. Other times I might hold it too long and outrun the curl. It's something you have to work out for yourself, and no amount of words can take the place of practice. The golden rule is bend the knees.

Modern multi fin surfboards are designed to be kept turning from rail to rail especially the twin fin which is very sluggish in a straight line but fast from edge to edge.

The amount of rail used in a turn is critical. A buried full rail, for example, is a speeding up manoeuvre close to the fall line which requires very little direction change. A very necessary manoeuvre for good surfing. A common mistake is that a lot of surfers try to turn the board too far around with too much rail in the water. The board slows down and they fall off. The simple rule is the greater the direction change you want the less rail in the water your need. But by the same token you will make your turn longer, more drawn out, and ultimately faster by using the rail to the fullest extent.

THE FOREHAND CUTBACK

The cutback is performed to bring the surfer back into the breaking part of the wave. It is a difficult manoeuvre because it is a pivot executed high in the critical part of the wave or a driving manoeuvre to get back to the curl. It

Above and left – *Richard Cram in full flight – A powerful cutback can be stopped almost anywhere along the track back to the curl.*

Right – *Mark Richards in a driving backside bottom turn – The pressure is now on the heels rather than toes.*

should always be negotiated with reference to the fall line. Initially the beginner should try it with minimum direction change, until he feels confident about the manoeuvre.

THE BACKHAND TURN

Totally different to a forehand turn, it is executed with your back to the wave, when you are never quite sure what the lip is doing. You bend your knees for the recoil effect the same as for a forehand turn, but the stance should be slightly different. Your feet should be almost parallel and at right angles to the inside rail and your weight pushed carefully back towards the face of the wave. I say carefully, because recovery at the end of the arc is the most difficult part of the whole process.

THE TOP TURN

This is a stall, or slowing down manoeuvre performed in the top part of the wave when it is too slow or weak to have any power at its base – simply a pivotal direction change to put you in a better position to run down the fall line. On conventional boards you need to stand closer to the tail for the board to pivot, but on some modern boards with hard edges you can turn anywhere on the face from virtually the same position. More on this when we discuss board design later.

TUBE RIDING

The times I've been suspended in the area between the wave face and the pitching lip of the wave as it breaks have been my most memorable surfing experiences. The tube is actually a tunnel of water, and a tube ride is like standing obscured from view behind a waterfall.

When you are surfing well enough to turn where you want and end up in the right position to trim down the fall line, sooner or later you will 'get tubed' whether by accident or design. It's the aim of most surfers on just about every wave to get into the tube and come out again. As the lip throws out above you, bend down and make your centre of gravity as low as possible. Draw your inside shoulder back while riding on your forehand. At first you will need a big wave with plenty of room inside the curl, keep your eyes open, watch the curl break and avoid the lip.

LAY BACK

This manoeuvre is only executed on your backhand and takes considerable practise and timing. When the wall is steep and the curl is coming over your head, lean over backwards like a limbo dancer and lay your back on the wall. In this position you have to relax and be supported by the wave face. Correcting by returning to an upright position is difficult and most surfers lose it at this stage.

Above – Tom Curren with a masterful top turn designed to slow the board up and change direction.

Above – *Marvin Foster at the Pipeline. The secret of success is pulling your trailing shoulder back parallel to the wave face, having your feet wide apart, and your eyes open.*

Left – *Greg Black at Narrabeen: the layback is one of the most dynamic methods of getting in the tube on your backhand.*

THE RE-ENTRY

If the surfboard is driven into a bottom turn too deep in the wave and meets the lip either half-way up or right at the top as it breaks, the manoeuvre is called a re-entry. This requires exceptionally good balance and a lot of luck during the split-second meeting with the lip. In fact the surfer instantly changes direction and heads back down the wave with the lip. If he reaches the top too early he will be left dangling, and if he gets there too late the lip will knock him off his board.

Beginners should practise this manoeuvre at a beach break with no other surfers about. Instead of getting off the wave before it finally closes out on the sandbank, turn off the bottom again and bounce off the white water coming in the other direction. With practice it can be a spectacular way to end your ride. Stay low as you come over with the white water and crouch and grab the rail if necessary to steady yourself in the foam.

The 'island pull out' is used often in modern surfing from deep in the tube. It you are unable to make it over the top without running the risk of being knocked back down with the lip, wait until the last couple of seconds before the wave closes over you. Grab the outside edge, bury the inside rail into the wall and let the fin break loose. The wave will pass over you, and you'll emerge behind it.

THE FLOATER

Essentially, the floater is a re-entry without direction. It is executed in the same position on the wave when it is about to close out. The Floater is delicate in that the board is moving very slowly and therefore is difficult to stand on. Practice is the key to this manoeuvre and timing is essential.

THE 360 LOOP

In the old days it was often dreamt of to do a carving 360 degree turn on the wave face but only rarely has this been achieved and never intentionally to my knowledge. However since the advent of modern multi fins the 360 loop can be done by most talented surfers. The action is similar to skateboard pivot turn except that the board is forced to pivot on the front rail high in the curl. Just as the wave breaks the fins break loose and the board follows around with the momentum of the wave and surfer.

Below – *Follow Robbie Bain's board's track – the 're-entry' or 'off the lip' involves driving hard out of a turn and bouncing off the broken section ahead.*

AERIALS

As surfing accelerates through the mid eighties and into the nineties no other manoeuvre points the direction of the future more clearly to me than the aerial. After all what other direction was there to go? It was inevitable that hot young grommets would take their skateboarding action with them onto the waves.

It seems like all good aerial surfers are, or have been, expert skateboarders. They first felt the weightlessness off the rim of a pool or launching off a ramp in the backyard for hour after hour until they conquered their fear and could relax in the air and think clearly about putting four wheels cleanly back on the ground.

The most basic aerial is called the "Ollie Pop" (in skate-boarding) and is the first step in taking to the air. The "Ollie Pop" can be performed on any part of the wave.

Steps to making the Ollie Pop:

1. Find the cross current in the wave. This can be done frontside or backside, as long as you find the cross currents to use as a launching point. You will find these currents coming up the face of the wave. A cross current can be recognized as a series of bumps coming up the face of the wave.
2. Use the cross current bump as a launching pad. As you hit the bump you let the weight off your front foot, until the nose of your board is in the air.
3. Then lift the weight off your back foot. At this point you will be in the air. Bring your weight front and centre to prepare to land.
4. To land you must use your knees and ankle's flexibility to absorb the shock of the landing. A stiff landing can cause your board to go under water and ruin the move.

The **'off-the-lip aerial'** is something altogether different from the "Ollie Pop". It depends more on speed and timing and is similar to a regular off the lip, except that you use the lip to project you up and over the face of the wave.

1. As you hit the lip of the wave you are compressing yourself to your board, keeping your centre of gravity low, and grabbing your outside rail. You should be in a vertical position with your back to the beach leaving yourself weightless.
2. The lip will launch you up and out of the wave, while at the same time you should be shifting your weight to bring yourself into an upright position. Keep your feet and board underneath you, but still in a compressed position.
3. When you are right above your board it is time to release your hand from your rail and expand your legs to absorb the landing. Be loose and flexible, just like the "Ollie Pop" landing. This completes your aerial.

Naturally the success of these manoeuvres depends on the water conditions at the time and your own instinct. It's not the getting air that is the most difficult part but a successful landing that takes a huge amount of practice and talent. At this time only a handful of surfers can repeatedly pull off aerials.

Air is happening in the 80's
Top – *Glen Winton*
Bottom – *Barton Lynch*

DUCK DIVE

The duck dive was originally used by kneeboard surfers whose boards used to have less buoyancy than the old Malibus but now with just as much foam in a surfboard as a kneeboard all experienced surfers use it as the most practical method of getting through the white water. While lying in a prone position paddling straight towards the white-water, rise up on your board to an extended push-up position, your hands holding the rails firmly. Now using your shoulder muscles plunge the nose downward under the broken wave. Follow this movement through with your body under the whitewater, kicking with your legs to submerge the board as deep as possible. When you are as deep as possible, push the ball of your foot into the deck on the tail of the board in order to make the nose head up towards the surface. About this time a good strong frog kick is a helpful means of getting you propelled in the right direction. This method takes a fair amount of timing and is really for experienced surfers, but with practise you will get it, perhaps try it in a swimming pool or still water first.

Above and right – *The duck dive showing the absolute efficiency of this manoeuvre to negotiate white water.*

Far right – *Even experienced surfers take a good look before paddling out in Hawaii.*

Surfing big waves

Opposite – *Hawaii's pipeline over 6' is another dimension.*

Left – *Early 60's, when men were men and boards were boards.*

RIDING large waves competently is possibly the most difficult and certainly the most challenging aspect of the surfing experience. Big surfable conditions are a rareity and only a handful of professionals have the opportunity to become proficient in riding them. They require an entirely different approach. Every honest surfer is both scared and respectful of their power, however learning to conquer your fear will make you a better surfer in all respects.

Waves over 2 metres should never be attempted by a novice. Don't even think about it until you feel totally confident in smaller waves. As you have probably realized by now it is difficult to use size alone to judge what is big

and small surf. A one metre wave can have more power than a two metre wave but in general when we think of big surf we are talking about over three metres.

Some surfers feel that riding big waves is just a matter of survival but this is not all there is to it. That is why some do it better than others and is also what separates the men from the boys. One good idea is to practice holding your breath. I remember doing this every night in the bath for weeks before my first trip to Hawaii and it really paid dividends.

On that first trip I also learnt to plan my attack carefully. Study the conditions in detail, get up high and take a good long look. It's a real matter of

NAT
'83 WAIMEA
photo: Sato

The author,
20' Waimea Bay.
The only way
out is to relax
and go with the
energy, even
when the whole
Pacific Ocean
caves in on you.

Nat at Waimea
photo: Sato

looking before you leap. Usually because the ocean is moving so dramatically during high surf all the action is taking place between two hundred metres to a mile from your vantage point. Watch for a good half hour letting one or two big sets roll through a full cycle showing up the rips and the impact zone. Sometimes what looks like smooth surface conditions from a distance are extremely bumpy in reality. Binoculars are a great help in picking up these important details. Generally big waves have reached their size because they have travelled so far at sea. The lulls in between the sets can be up to 10 minutes. It's handy to time the arrival of the bigger sets. Use your judgement to pick up a reference point directly in front of the ideal take-off. Use a big tree or house – something that will stand out when you are looking from the line-up towards the shore.

Probably the hardest thing to remember is to consciously slow down, not to rush, spend a little more time waxing your board, doing some stretching exercises, realizing that this is the time you need every little thing possible going for you. Usually there will be a vicious shore break associated with big surf so don't go charging into the mouth of the lion, wait until the set has passed and then move swiftly through this critical area. Once you are safely in the inevitable rip keep paddling solidly making every stroke count. Don't use up more energy than necessary although at times it will seem like you are not getting anywhere.

Once you are in the line-up look around for that house or tree you were going to use as a reference point. Position yourself directly in front of it and sit up keeping your eyes glued to the horizon. When you see the set approaching start to paddle out. As a general rule you should let the first set go as it will show you exactly where they are breaking. When you decide to ride one of the set waves, let the first one go as it cleans up the surface chop after the lull and the second and third waves are more often than not a fair bit bigger.

When you decide that this one will be yours, concentrate on its form – throw one glance to your reference point on the shore and correct if necessary while starting to paddle for the wave. Use all your available resources of energy to catch the wave and don't stand up too late or too early but use your timing to get into a low crouch to take the drop on take-off just as the wave breaks. This is the most critical point in all surfing, when most mistakes are made, so have confidence, just do it right, absorbing the bumps and drops as you let the board run down the face, all the way to the bottom. Naturally this depends on the wave you are riding but most big waves have a clearly defined pattern either telling you to go all the way to the bottom before you turn or angling immediately you get to your feet. As I said on most big waves the easier route is directly to the bottom and start your bottom turn slow by rolling the rail up and applying pressure. This is where you should be slow and positive. Don't make it a blatant, jerky move, just strong steady force to carve a turn away from the curl. How far you run the turn depends on the wave and your ability. If you want to just survive you should run the board for the shoulder as quickly as possible – more experienced big wave riders will stay closer to the curl flirting with the

Sunset Beach. It is this sight that strikes awe into the heart of every surfer who visits Hawaii.

power, flaunting their ability against the intensity of the situation.

It is almost a certainty that you will get nailed by the curl, pearl on take-off or make some minor mistake that will make your first big wave experience a memorable one. Don't be daunted, it happens to everyone. A wipe out in big surf is once again a matter of slowing down and going with it. Whatever you do don't panic and fight the power of the ocean. You will never win. Let the force of the wave push you anywhere it wants, just give up and go with the flow. I sometimes think of a cork in a washing machine. It helps me to put it in perspective. Just like the cork, eventually you will come to the surface. As you are being propelled towards the bottom it's important to open your eyes, usually big waves are breaking on reefs so try to keep your hands up to protect your head from hitting the reef. Nine times out of ten you are back in a boil and the force of the lip hits the floor cushioning your impact with the bottom. Eventually the force will subside and you can look up and start swimming for the surface. Quite likely there will be some turbulant boils. Don't swim into these but pick your way around them. It's easy with your eyes open.

When you reach the surface take in that breath of air you have been wanting for ages and make it a big one because the chances are you are right in the impact zone with another wave about to break. If so, dive as quick and deep as possible, anchoring yourself to the reef with your hands and only coming up when you can see that the boils have subsided. The next important thing to remember is to stay in the white water. Instinct tells you to get out of the breaking wave area and into the rip but this can be a fatal mistake. **Stay in the white water.** It will wash you with it towards the beach, so just relax, diving under each wave as it washes over you.

EQUIPMENT

In the early days of riding mountains, huge 4 metre long heavy single fin boards called Elephant guns were used exclusively. Today modern big wave surfers prefer long, narrower versions of their short wave boards complete with multi fins and bright paint jobs. There is a certain advantage in having extra weight, either with more fibreglass or a thicker centre stringer. This gives a bit more momentum and more importantly makes it significantly stronger and therefore less susceptible to breaking under the stress of a big wave. I always use a leg rope because if the wave is big enough it will break it like a piece of cotton.

Surfing big waves is really a special feeling and as soon as you have experienced your heart leaping into your mouth on the take-off the gee force pushing you through the board on a bottom turn or the adrenalin being pumped through your system after a terrifying ride, you will know the feeling I am talking about.

Top – Mark Richards taking the drop at Waimea Bay.

Above – Hans Hedeman. The Pipeline demands that you go right to the bottom before the first turn.

Left – Ken Bradshaw and Simon Anderson equipment for 15' Sunset (84-85 World Cup) Ken 7'6", Simon 7'8".

Competitive Surfing

The rookie can still beat the champ. Mark Occhilupo, first in the 1985 Beaurepaires, world champion Tom Carroll second.

THE good thing about surfing is that you can become as involved in it as you like. The scope is there for you to make it a complete way of life, or just a pleasant recreation. The competitive aspect of surfing is a great experience, but never lose sight of the fact that surfing is really all about riding an ocean wave. This is something I've tried to keep in mind throughout my surfing career whether surfing in contests or for my own enjoyment, winning or losing. But, of course, there are times when you can successfully combine competition and the sheer exhilaration of surfing; times when you are wired to perform well, to cut loose but retain that necessary element of control. I still have vivid memories of my first big competitive success in 1963. It was quite a rush.

I was fifteen, still at school and living with my parents in our old gabled home on the beachfront at Collaroy. A few days before the Australian titles were to be held at Bondi I cut my foot open on a broken bottle as I ran up the beach before school. While the doctor sewed five stitches into my foot I quizzed him about the best way to support the injury so I could still surf. For me it was no ordinary contest. I was Australian Junior Champion and

still eligible to compete in the junior division for some years, but an all expenses paid trip to America had been offered to the winner of the open men's and I was determined to compete in it. The injury kept me out of the surf for the rest of that week but nothing could stop me taking to the water that weekend at Bondi. Not even a heavily bandaged and painful foot. I made it through to the final and I can remember waiting for that one last wave I needed to show my ability to the utmost. It came, not big, but a strong and long-walled wave. I pulled the board off the bottom, lying prone until the last second to ease the strain on my foot and keep the stitches in place. The wave was a ripper and I won the contest.

Organized competitive surfing in Australia as we know it today started with the formation of the Australian Surfing Association in 1963. It is a strictly amateur organization set up originally to give a united voice to a bunch of highly individual characters who were having to cope with bureaucratic intervention (e.g. council surfboard registration and beach pollution). These days the national body's main function is to administer to the State and area affiliates and run the Australian titles annually. Within your

Above – *All eyes on Burleigh for the annual Stubbies Pro contest.*
Right – *Preparing for battle – man on man.*

area there are one or two surfing clubs and these have affiliation with the A.S.A. These surfing clubs are usually pretty loose affairs with plenty of fun social activity and inter-club competition and they provide a means of entering the State and National championships. There are seven divisions of amateur competition: cadets (under 15), junior (under 19), open, senior mens (28 and over), masters (over 35), kneeboard and womens.

They also administer a school surfing competition divided into under 19, 17 and 15 years of age, as well as kneeboards and girls. What happens is that the six best surfers from their area get invited to compete in the State titles, the winners going on to represent the State in the Nationals.

The only amateur association operating independently of the A.S.A. is within the school system. Individual schools have contests to pick their two best surfers who represent them in the area competition and hopefully go on to the State and National teams challenge. The schools foster the idea of team spirit which is usually not associated with surfing but has obvious validity in pride of school and establishing good relationships with other individuals who share a common interest.

Universities have similar set-ups designed to continue after high school competition.

Many surfers find that humble beginnings in small contests spur them on to surf better and develop a more aggressive approach in the water, and these days with so many people surfing, aggression is often the only way to get a wave. Narrabeen in Sydney is a good example. Here every day is a competition and the general standard of surfing is accordingly higher than at most other beaches. Of course, there are those surfers who regard this 'rat race' approach to surfing as hearsay, but I take neither side. When I was a kid I thrived on competition, but many of the finest surfers I have known have never entered a contest. Recreational or competitive surfing? It's purely up to the individual, but in this chapter we're going to take a look at the latter.

JUDGING

The judging of surfing has had a difficult childhood. The main problem has always been that the judges' interpretation of events in the water is what counts, no matter what system is used. In the earliest contests a panel of surfers simply watched the whole event and chose a winner. This method had its share of problems even when it was refined to a point score out of twenty. Judges were frequently accused of bias and of favouring certain styles. And there was an element of truth in this. The fashionable style of surfing at any given time did become the fashionable style of judging. One person's way of surfing became the measure of what was good, and heaven help you if you didn't conform.

Surfing still has the same problem today, although the professional attitudes of today's top surfers and the large amounts of money riding on the results have brought some sophistication to judging methods. New sys-

Above – *Victory for a triumphant Rabbit Bartholomew.*
Right – *Martin Potter off the lip. In professional competition the only way to win is to push yourself beyond your limits.*

Competition involves more pressure than recreational surfing. Cut loose, but try not to blow it!

tems are being tested all the time, but one of the most significant in recent years was the system introduced for the first Stubbies Classic on the Gold Coast in March, 1977. Devised by Peter Drouyn, a veteran competitor himself, it centred around there being only two surfers in the water at a time, free to do their own thing. The five judges scored points out of ten for such things as style and co-ordination, aggression, close-to-the-wall manoeuvring, split-second positioning, and the way in which each surfer used the wave to its fullest extent. Points were also given to the surfer who won each battle of wits to gain possession of a wave. More recent development in the 'man on man' method of judging has been the use of a priority buoy where the first surfer to round it has wave selection.

The old drop in rule is still in effect. The surfer who gets to his feet first (closest to the curl) has wave priority. But with the advent of professionalism the pros have been clever enough to engineer their opponents into a drop in position, eliminating them from the contest as the surfer who has a drop in scored against him or her cannot possibly win the heat. This problem is particularly difficult when surfing a peak with a left and a right hander. Who is to say which surfer is on the inside?

Up until the introduction of Drouyn's system, the most advanced method of judging had been the 'objective' system, in which surfers were given points for each manoeuvre executed. Under this system a number of manoeuvres are defined before the contest begins and points allocated to

each. For example, a small turn might be worth one point, a 360 degree loop worth 500 points. In the Coke/2SM Surfabout each judge allocates points for one surfer's ride, then the judging sheets are rotated to eliminate any claim of bias. Recently compromise systems have been introduced which include points for an 'interpretive' or 'subjective' score, as well as points for manoeuvres. Another variant is 'wave size', in which a wave size category is decided upon at the beginning of a round and maintained throughout the round. This simply means that the surfer who takes bigger waves has the opportunity to score in a higher range.

Objective judging was first used for the Hang Ten contest in Hawaii. It works quite well providing the waves are good and consistent. But this is the problem for all systems and all surfing contests. Accurate judging in poor conditions is a difficult task. If not altogether impossible, it is surely only a matter of time before the video camera is put to its best use and used for recording the individual performance. This can then be judged by judges who are being paid for their time, having already served an apprenticeship to qualify them for the job then they can give an informed professional decision. Professional contests already make use of these developments as well as a computerised scoreboard.

TURNING PRO

Several contests around the world are now Pro/Am involving both profes-

Narrabeen circa 1960. Every keen surfer in Sydney turned out for the first big contest.

sional and amateur surfers. This is the only way a hot young surfer can get a crack at the big time and turn professional. It is important that this decision is not made without giving thought to the consequence of the action because once you openly accept money for your place in a contest you are considered a professional and the decision is irreversible in that you will not be allowed in amateur competition again for two years. The only way you can avoid being classed as a full professional when you are starting to compete on the circuit is by paying your winnings into the trust account of your States A.S.A. You only have access to these funds for legitimate travel expenses incured in the pursuit of your pro surfing career. This system allows you to find out what its like being a pro surfer and still maintain your amateur status.

Being a professional is not all give on the sponsors side with you just surfing away without a care in the world – it's an obligation – there are no free lunches as the saying goes, sponsorship is a two way street with the sponsor out to get the best deal possible for his product. If you are talented enough to be offered free surfboards, clothing or financial assistance, realize that the company has to recoup that cost from the gross sales figures of which only a slight proportion is given to advertising (which is what you are). It's a narrow path where you can't go around beating a big drum singing the virtues of your sponsor's product but you can make sure you ride or wear the product under every circumstance possible, conducting yourself with humility and dignity. Always behaving like a professional and keeping a close watch on your pride and your mouth. If you are having a problem with the fit or performance of the board call and make an appointment to see your sponsor, explain the problem and nine times out of ten you will work out something beneficial to both sides, and more importantly, in a professional manner.

THE PRO CIRCUIT

The circuit has undergone an incredible burst of growth over the past few years. In 87/88 the pro surfer who wishes to compete in every rated event around the world will have to travel almost continuously, living out of a suitcase for 11 months of the year.

The circuit begins in Japan with the A rated ($33,000) Mauri Cup on Nijima Island. Next comes the A rated Gotcha Pro at Sandy Beach in Hawaii. In South Africa there are two A rated events, one in Cape Town and the other in Durban. Next it's off to California U.S.A. for the A rated Stubbies in Oceanside and the AA ($60,000) OP Pro at Huntington Beach. Come August the pros are all in Europe. France has three A rated events and there is one in Cornwall, England. Brazil has an A rated event in September, just before getting back to Japan for another AA.

There are three A rated events in Australia on this leg of the tour. One is Western Australia, another on the Gold Coast in Queensland and the BHP in Newcastle, just north of Sydney. As December is peak big wave season in Hawaii there are three prestigious A rated events on the north shore of Oahu. The new year starts with an A rated event in Santa Cruz, California and the Australian Grand Slam around Easter, The Bells contest in Victoria and the Coke in Sydney.

STANDARD FORMAT SHEET
32 MAN ON MAN

ROUND ONE		ROUND TWO	QUARTER FINALS	SEMI FINALS	FINAL
1	TOM CARROLL 1 / NICKY WOOD 32	1			
2	JOE ENGEL 16 / MIKE BURNESS 17	1			
3	GLEN WINTON 8 / GARY ELKERTON 25	2			
4	BARTON LYNCH 9 / MITCH THORSON 24			1	
5	MARTIN POTTER 4 / S. BEDFORD-BROWN 29	3			
6	GREG DAY 13 / DENTON MIYAMURA 20	2			
7	HANS HEDEMAN 5 / ROB BAIN 28	4			
8	RICHARD CRAM 12 / MATT KECHELE 21				
9	TOM CURREN 2 / GREG BROWN 31	5			
10	KINGSLEY LOOKER 15 / MIKE LAMBRESI 18	3			
11	WES LAINE 7 / MIKE NEWLING 26	6			
12	WAYNE BARTHOLOMEW 10 / BRYCE ELLIS 23			2	
13	CHEYNE HORAN 3 / CRAIG COMEN 30	7			
14	TERRY RICHARDSON 14 / SIMON ANDERSON 19	4			
15	MARK OCCHILUPO 6 / NICK CARROLL 27	8			
16	MICHAEL HO 11 / GRAHAM WILSON 22				

Left – *Typical breakdown of man on man format.*
Above – *Politicians love the high profile associated with professional sport. L to R: Barton Lynch, Bob Hawke, Tom Carroll.*

Above – *Young Cronulla surfer Mark Occhilupo on his first wave in the 1985 Pipeline Masters Contest.*

Right – *The direction of pro surfing? One event in the '85 pro circuit was held in a wave pool, in Allentown, Pennsylvania. It does not look like it will ever replace the real thing.*

Pam Burridge and Tom Carroll. Professional surfing is a rapidly expanding career for talented ladies.

Total prize money for the year is $760,000 which is distributed primarily to the top sixteen placegetters. Naturally, competition for the top sixteen is fierce, it takes so much work to get there and even more to maintain position. This coveted group are automatically seeded in the second round at all the contests avoiding the chance of elimination in the trials.

The top sixteen is where the battle for who will be crowned World Champion takes place. Points are allocated for each place in every contest on the circuit. The final placings are counted from the accumulated points. However, in order to allow for injury, ill health, or other personal reasons, the competitors are allowed to miss four events.

Naturally, when you are first making moves towards turning pro you are not expected to compete in A and AA events. There is a healthy number of B and C contests which are Pro/Am but still carry purses for the aspiring young pro.

HINTS FOR CONTESTANTS

1 The winner, as in all games, is the won who plays best by the rules. Read the rules carefully.
2 Study the surf before you go out in your heat. Try to anticipate just where you would be going on each wave and whether, depending on conditions, it would be better to ride your waves all the way to the beach or to concentrate on one large and difficult section.
3 Wear a watch. In all contests there is either a time or wave-count factor. You may have thirty minutes or thirty waves, but in either case it is handy to know how long you've been in the water.
4 Look for the bigger waves. It is easier to accumulate points when there is more wave face to play with. Keep an eye on the horizon and be prepared to get off a bad wave if you see something better coming.
5 Don't interfere with any other surfer. Usually the inside man has right of way but you generally know when you're in the wrong. Be aggressive but keep within the rules. The surfer who is in command of the situation usually wins.
6 Make sure you have the right board for the conditions on the day. Most professionals have two or three boards with them at all times – one for small and sloppy waves (usually wide and flat-bottomed like a skateboard) a standard board for waves from 1 to 3 metres, and a gun with lots of bottom curve to hold it into waves from 3 to 5 metres.

Remember a ride is judged from the minute your hands leave the board so don't get up until you are sure the wave is worth it.

Hawaiian pro Reno Abellira summed it up perfectly when he was interviewed after placing second in the 1977 Coke contest. Asked why his equipment was so different from the other boards on the beach, he explained that after four trips to Australia he had definite ideas about what boards he needed to meet the conditions. 'All these guys are so close in ability that having the right board can make all the difference.'

Above – *Kingsley Looker coming off the top with power to burn.*

Following pages Left – *Mark Richards showing his incredible ability to hold down a twin fin.*

Right – *Michael Ho at the Pipeline. Grabbing the rail is back in vogue again because the risk of wiping-out is minimized.*

Waves and Weather

Quality beachbreak is desired by all surfers from beginners to experts.

EVERYTHING you do on a surfboard is controlled by the wave you are riding. People who don't surf often seem incapable of understanding that waves can vary considerably in size and shape from one beach to the next on the same day. Usually this is because they don't understand the variables involved – wind and swell direction, the tide, the shape of the sandbank or reef; so many things that knowing where to go at the right time is as hard as learning to stand up on a surfboard. But a study of the weather in relation to surfing conditions can be interesting, particularly when it results in you being in the right place at the right time when the waves are good.

It seems fitting here that we discuss just what it is that constitutes good surf. Different surfers often prefer different conditions, but you'll find them unanimous in their approval if the surf is described as '2 to 3 metres, hot and glassy'. Now what does that mean? Two to three metres is a description of

the height of the wave, from trough to peak. A little over the head of the rider but not really big enough to be dangerous. 'Hot' usually refers to the quality of the swell. A hot wave stands up cleanly when it hits a sandbank point or reef and runs away in one direction or another. 'Glassy' is a description applied to ideal water surface conditions, which occur when there is no wind.

To have good waves you must have a good swell. There are two types of swell; ground and wind. Both are produced by wind but the ground swell originates in the open ocean, often a thousand kilometres or more from the shore on which it eventually breaks. It is generally the better type to ride because of the uniformity gained in its long march to shore. You can identify a ground swell by the longer distance between waves. I've also noticed that ground swells often produce sets of ten waves. Australia's east coast rarely gets ground swell but it is frequent on the south and west coasts.

Hawaii rarely gets anything but ground swell, generated by huge storms off the Aleutian Islands near Alaska. California also gets these same swells, but by then they have usually lost much of their power and size.

Wind swells are generated by local wind conditions. On the Australian east coast, for example, our predominant winter wind is the southerly which gives us consistent south swell. In summer the nor'easter is the prevailing wind and we get north-east swell which is usually choppy with waves close together because they have travelled such a short distance. Hence there is very little line to summer waves in Sydney and they break unpredictably.

The next variable is wind direction. The best wind for surfing blows off the land. An offshore wind removes chop from the wave face and holds the waves up for longer before they break, making for a steeper ride. An onshore wind, on the other hand, makes the surface choppy and causes the waves to break sooner than they should. Light onshore winds don't make much difference, but over 10 or 12 knots the surf becomes 'blown-out'. Light winds are more pleasant to surf in, as strong winds make it difficult to control the board.

The shape of the ocean floor plays a big part in determining surfing conditions. The ideal bottom shape is a triangle gradually tapering into deeper

Above – *Submerged reefs break with abundant power as the swell is tripped entering shallower water.*
Right – *Point surf usually breaks very close to the headland and are characteristically hard-breaking waves.*

water on all sides. Such a set-up would produce perfect lefts and rights down either side with a swell coming in at 90 degrees to its apex. Unfortunately perfect set-ups are rare, and because wind and waves erode the shoreline in this manner, they never last for long. Surfing breaks are caused by three physical formations: the reef (submerged rock); the point (usually round stones); and the sandbank.

REEF SURF

Breaks on either rock or coral base. Reef waves are characteristically hard-breaking, strong waves which stand up abruptly where the reef begins. Not for beginners. A fall onto a shallow reef can result in serious injury. They are not particularly good learning waves anyway. They break consistently in the same spot which makes them ideal for experts but lacking in the variety needed for first lessons. They generally have a tapering wall that changes the wave's shape and direction as it moves around the reef.

POINT SURF

Another dangerous area for the beginner but a delight for the competent surfer. Most point breaks are made of round stones, rounded by countless years of wave action, which extended from the base of the headland for some distance into the water. The waves usually break very close to the rocks. Even then, until you are familiar with the break, you should use the angled take-off, paddling away from the curl.

BEACH BREAK

The most common type of surf. It is a sandbar which changes constantly with wind and swell conditions, and it can be the best and worst kind of wave to surf, depending on how much the sandbar resembles that perfect triangle. Beach breaks are definitely the best places to learn. They can throw up so many different waves every time you go in the water. Often there are shifting peaks with waves jumping up in front of you as you paddle out. You need to be a quick and agile paddler to surf beach breaks well.

TIDES

Point, reef and beach breaks are all affected by the tide to some degree,

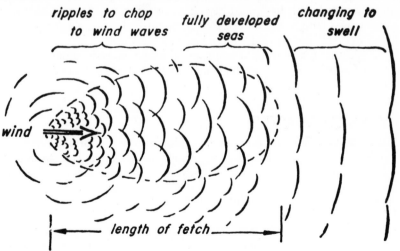

Wind creates waves. The further away from the storm's centre the more even the swell will become.

83

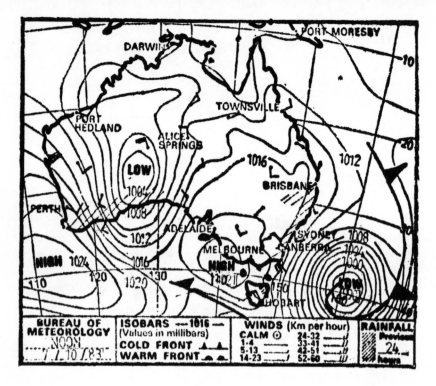

A low pressure area in the Tasman Sea brings south swell and wind to N.S.W.

depending on the size and direction of the swell. As a general rule I go surfing just as the tide has gone low and is starting to rise. As the tide comes up the waves tend to build in size. High tide usually makes them full and slower to break. But, as I said, this is only a general rule.

The weather maps in the newspapers and on television are good references for noting the times for high and low tides. By observing conditions at your break as the tide changes you should be able to pick the times when the waves will be best.

TYPES OF WAVES

HOLLOW WAVES: Not for beginners. Hollow waves look like barrels or cylinders from the side, and they are the most sought after waves by expert surfers because they are best for riding the tube. To ride them you stay low and drop all the way to the bottom. If you try to cut along the top of a hollow wave you run the risk of free-falling out of the face.

FLAT FACE: These are found in areas where the Continental Shelf is gradual and the swell is slowed down by increasing contact with the ocean floor before it reaches the shore. Flat waves break slowly and with very little power. They are good for beginners to practise balance and turning, but the move up to more challenging waves should be made as soon as possible.

Both hollow and flat waves and all the waves in between have one more

variable – thickness. Thickness is determined by a combination of bottom shape and the depth of the water. A thin wave breaks over a gradual slope (like the Continental Shelf) where the base of the swell is slowed down causing the top to come down evenly. Thin waves are less critical and more fun. You can even stick your head or shoulder in the curl without taking a pounding.

A thick wave comes out of deep water to break (usually on a submerged reef) with full force. Thick waves should be avoided by the novice because they require accurate timing to avoid the thick lip that so often breaks bodies and boards.

There are also two ways in which a swell can present itself. Depending on the swell's consistency the waves might be 'lined up' or just 'peaking'. Ground swells usually produce lined up conditions where the waves stretch for long distances along the beach. In conditions like this, reefs and points work best, because few sandbanks can hold 'lined up' swell conditions.

Peaks are generally a beach break phenomenon, and when they break on a constant sandbank they are good waves for beginners, allowing plenty of room to escape the curl.

Weather maps can be an accurate guide to surfing conditions if you know how to read them. Weather patterns are made up of high and low pressure systems. In a high pressure area the wind travels in an anti-clockwise direction; in a low pressure area in a clockwise direction. Swells can be generated by both highs and lows, but lows usually produce bigger and better waves. The best conditions occur when the low stays off the coast. If it comes too close, wind, rain, storms and unpredictable surf usually result, but if the low keeps a safe distance out to sea and travels parallel to the coast, surfers can reap benefits without suffering the bad weather.

High pressure systems usually bring good weather but few waves, except in areas where storm swells frequently pass out at sea and the anti-clockwise winds blow off the land.

The circles you see around the pressure systems on your weather map are isobars, which indicate the intensity of the system and the area it covers. There is usually a number marked in the centre of the system. The lower number the more intense the system.

Left – These two pictures show how dramatically wind effects the quality of the surf.

Below – Tropical cyclone or low off the Queensland coast usually produces good north swell down the East Coast.

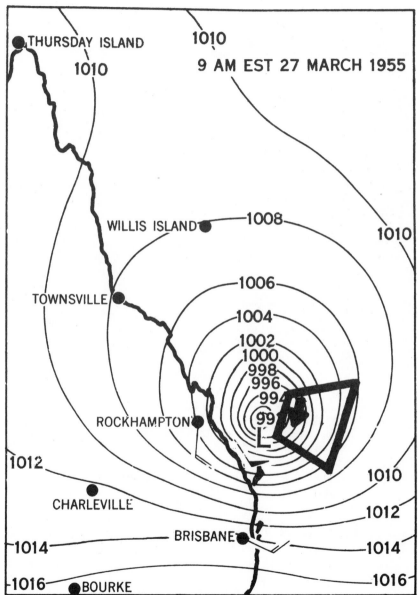

THURSDAY ISLAND

1010

1010

9 AM EST 27 MARCH 1955

WILLIS ISLAND — 1008

1010

1006

TOWNSVILLE

1004

1002
1000
998
996
994
99

ROCKHAMPTON

1012

1010

CHARLEVILLE

1012

BRISBANE

1014

1014

1016 BOURKE

1016

Where the Waves are

THROUGHOUT the year different parts of the world have good surf, some better than others. In twenty-five years of surfing I've travelled the world five times and found good waves in some pretty unusual places, as well as some familiar ones. Here are some of them.

AUSTRALIA

NORTH COAST, NOOSA HEADS: This is the northernmost part of the east coast with predictable quality waves. It has five point breaks – Main Beach, Johnsons, National Park, Ti Tree and Granite Bay. All of these are rights which work from 1 to 3 metres, depending on the amount of sand built up in the bays. Noosa can break at any time, but it is consistent during cyclone season (December to March). Anyone who has experienced a cyclone swell at Noosa riding on one wave for over 200 metres at National Park has had one of surfing's true pleasures.

GOLD COAST: Has two exceptional breaks, Kirra and Burleigh Heads. Up until a few years ago Currumbin also fell into that category, but government development has interfered with the estuary and the waves are no longer the same. Burleigh is the only spot on the Gold Coast that accepts a south or south-east swell, and whenever it breaks it provides one of the fastest and hollowest right-hand waves in the world. It is an extremely hard place to surf, with entry from the rocks often difficult. Kirra takes a north or east swell, often associated with a cyclonic depression. Sand-stabilising break-waters have been built and more by luck than good management, the consistency of the waves is better than it ever was.

BYRON BAY: The most easterly point in Australia has three magnificent breaks which offer surf on any wind. Again, the quality is dependent on the sand movement. The Pass is a point break with a build-up of sand over volcanic rock. It works best with an east swell and southerly winds. If the wind is from the west, Wategoes Beach, directly below the Cape Byron lighthouse is worth checking. On the other side, facing south, is Tallows. In summer the accumulated sand from winter storms and the prevailing north-east wind makes for incredible lefts – a rare treat on the north coast. A few kilometres south of Byron Bay is Broken Head, to my mind a unique wave. It seems to almost stand still, but it is so hollow. Broken works best on north swells but it will also fire on an east swell, with the wind anywhere from west to south. It too depends on sand movement for its quality, but three big rock formations just off shore stop the sand from moving past the point.

LENNOX HEAD: Another ten kilometres down the coast is Lennox head, a fine wave when it works. Rounded stones form the base of this powerful right-hand point wave. Sand builds up on the rocks but Lennox is more dependent on swell than sand movement. The swell must be south or south-east and the wind from the same direction. Because it is on the outside edge of a vast bay it picks up the south swell extremely well, making it the most consistent wave in winter on the north coast.

ANGOURIE: The next point break worthy of special mention. Although surf abounds in the Yamba area, much of it is accessible only by four-wheel drive vehicles. Angourie on the other hand is an easy-to-get-to surfing paradise with rounded stones over a rock shelf that needs only a little swell to break. It works best on a north swell but will fire on an east. South swell tend to close out over 2 metres and the wave is usually short.

CRESCENT HEAD: Situated twenty-two kilometres from Kempsey, an excellent wave in a north to east swell with south to south-west winds. Those winds are common in winter but the swell direction not so. In the early days Crescent was surfed on any swell but these days its south swell waves are less attractive.

CENTRAL COAST: There is a lot of good surf in the area between Newcastle and Gosford. Forresters Beach north of Terrigal is the big wave spot, with a submerged reef 100 metres offshore, which produces good lefts on big east or south-east swells with north-west to west winds. Further down the coast Box Head near Ocean Beach has a long-running left-hander over a sandbar. Swell direction is critical because the break is inside the mouth of Brisbane Waters and will not break in anything but a south-east swell. Winds must be north to north-east.

SYDNEY: On the northside Narrabeen is the most consistent break. It works on both north and south swells with the wind from west to north-east. Best conditions are north swell and north wind.

On the southside of Sydney is Cronulla, an area that must have been extremely beautiful before the advent of terracotta tile roofs and ticky tacky home units. Cronulla Point is a rock shelf onto which south to east swells pound consistently. When the swell is over 2 metres you can take off outside the shelf and set up a good long ride. Wind should be south to south-west but it can be ridden – with an exceptionally critical take-off – in south-east conditions. At the other end of Cronulla, Voodoo provides an excellent, and often under-estimated, left-hander. North-east wind with south swell required.

SOUTH COAST: South of Wollongong all the way to the Victorian border there are numerous good right and left reef breaks. 'Pipeline' or Wreck Bay near Jervis Bay is an amazing left-hand reef break on a south swell and north-east wind, and there are several quality breaks around Ulladulla.

VICTORIA: North-east of Melbourne, Phillip Island has some good breaks. Flynns Reef is an excellent right and Cat Bay often produces good lefts. On the other side of Port Phillip Bay, near Torquay, is Bells Beach, home of the

Surf Stoked. When Little Rincon at Victoria's Bells Beach is pumping it's enough to blow your mind!

annual Easter surfing contest. It is not a particularly hollow wave but it is extremely powerful during the autumn and winter months. I don't think I'll ever forget the first time I saw Bells. I was fifteen and had travelled to Victoria with some other surfers to compete in the second Bells contest. We awoke to an amazing sight – lines of swell all the way to the horizon. I've seen Bells like that many times since. It's an old-fashioned wave, in that it doesn't really suit modern in-the-tube surfing. The best way to surf it is to pick off sections, wind down the line with no worries about the wave closing out because it rarely breaks all the way to the bottom and you can surf around the curl.

THE BIGHT: Australia's southern coastline joining west and east has some of the most terrifying waves in the world. The breaks are too numerous to mention here, but all the way from Port Campbell to Albany in Western Australia there is good surf. The desolate Cactus area on the edge of the Nullarbor Plain has three excellent reef breaks – Caves, good from 1 to 3 metres; Castles, good from 2 to 4 metres; and Cactus itself, good up to 2 metres.

WEST AUSTRALIA: Margaret River, 200 kilometres south of Perth is the most famous and consistent wave, but all along the southern coastline are submerged reefs jutting out into the ocean. With the right swell and wind direction all are capable of producing quality surf. Autumn is the best season. North of Perth is still virtually undiscovered territory.

BALI

From March to September Bali is a paradise for surf, although the island has changed in recent years with the influx of tourists. But most of the island people have maintained their unique culture and the waves keep rolling in. The surf starts right where you jump off the plane. The airport runway is built right on the extremity of Kuta Reef, and as the plane wings in over Uluwatu you can often see the long lines of swell pouring through. There is plenty of cheap accommodation at Kuta Beach or nearby Legian and the island's reef breaks are all within a short distance. It should be mentioned here that Bali's reef breaks are dangerous and not for the novice surfer. Swell hits both sides of the island from March to September and, depending on wind conditions, you can get good waves whenever you want them. Uluwatu is the best surf break, a long, grinding left that breaks from 1 to 4 metres with the ideal size around 2 to 3 metres. It breaks over sharp coral and precautions must be taken if you suffer a cut, or a nasty saltwater ulcer will result. Kuta Reef is another powerful left that should never be underestimated, while Kuta Beach has several good beach breaks where you can relax when you tire of full on surfing. On the opposite side of the island, directly in front of the Bali Beach Hotel is Sanur, a strong and long-walled right-hander.

MAURITIUS

The same ocean conditions that send huge swells pouring into the Great Australian Bight, also create good waves on the other side of the Indian

Angourie: The N.S.W. North Coast has many perfect point breaks.

Ocean, in Mauritius. In autumn Tamarin Bay, twenty-five kilometres across the island from Port Louis, produces beautiful, hollow left-handers over a reef. Lamorne is another quality wave on the island.

SOUTH AFRICA

Autumn and winter are the best times of year, but you will need a warm wetsuit and rubber gloves and booties. During the mid-sixties travelling surfers from California discovered surf at Jefferies Bay, 100 kilometres south of Port Elizabeth on the east coast. Jefferies is not unlike Burleigh Heads in that it is a point with sand covering a rock shelf providing a consistent wave base. In 1967 Wayne Lynch, Ted Spencer and I surfed Jefferies for three weeks while we were making 'Sea of Joy' with Australian surf film-maker Paul Witzig. Mostly there are two distinct breaks – Tubes and Super Tubes. Luckily we had good waves at Super Tubes that ran right through into Tubes and finally closed out down on the beach break. Durban has good surf on occasions during this same period and Cape Town has excellent surf.

NORTH AFRICA

As you head up the west coast of Africa towards Europe the surf is simply wherever you find it. Senegal has good waves on a reef at the entrance to Dakar harbour. Morocco has plenty of good surf. I have surfed only as far south as Casablanca but I have heard there are many good breaks beyond. My best waves were had at Kenitra between November and February when

By far the most consistent quality wave in Sydney.

Right – *Clean swell is a tell-tail sign. Find a good bank and surf your brains out.*
Below – *South Africa's Jefferies Bay 2m to 2½m and pumping.*

*Uluwatu, Bali: The sight that greets every lucky surfer after
a long walk from the main road.*

Above – *The fabulous Rincon. Queen of the Californian coast.*
Right – *Classic Californian tube. The kelp in the background helps keep the water glassy all day.*

it is too cold to surf in Europe. Off the coast of Morocco the Canary Islands has a number of good breaks shared by very few surfers. Best in the northern winter months.

EUROPE

The idea in this part of the world is to surf as far north as possible during the late summer. Biarritz in France has excellent waves in September and October, but by November it is time to head south to the warmer climate of Spain and Portugal.

The surfing area of France extends south from Bordeaux to the Spanish border. Hossegor, twenty-five kilometres north of Biarritz has a series of excellent sandy points that hold their shape up to 3 metres, and there are good waves on both sides of the mouth of the Adour River. La Barre on the southern side used to be the best surf in France but since the extension of a breakwater there is no longer the same sand buildup as at Boucau on the northern side. The beach breaks around Biarritz itself are quite good but further south towards Spain at Guethary a large submerged reef holds waves from 2 to 4 metres. Lafittania is a right-hand reef break another kilometre south which produces the most consistent waves in France from 1 to 3 metres. As you cross the France-Spanish border there is a picturesque rivermouth break called Hendaye which has excellent waves and a beautiful view of the Pyrenees.

Along the northern coastline of Spain there are numerous rivermouth breaks that all seem to produce good waves on the incoming tide. Portugal has a series of good left-hand breaks just south of Porto and reefs and rivermouths all the way down to Lisbon. At the river entrance near Lisbon there is a good left-hand break at Estoril.

THE UNITED STATES

CALIFORNIA: The rebirth of modern surfing began here and there are

excellent breaks both north and south of Los Angeles. The best known Los Angeles break is Malibu, setting for a dozen Hollywood beach epics and where Bob Simmons experimented in surfboard design using the almost perfectly regimented south swells. The west coast is lucky with its surfing conditions; in summer it receives south swells, in winter north swells, and year-round kelp beds keep the wind off the waves.

North of Malibu is Secos, Country Line and another Californian surfing mecca, Rincon. Many times I have paddled out at the outside point (Indicator) here on a good-sized north swell in winter and punched down the line like a freight train. Further north is Hammonds Reef, Gaviota and The Ranch, once privately owned but recently divided into many smaller estates. It is the most condensed surfing paradise I have ever seen, with numerous good breaks in a small area. Razorback is my favorite, but Rights and Lefts, Point Conception and Drakes are all incredible waves, a little too powerful for the average surfer.

One hundred and fifty kilometres or so further north Santa Cruz has a long, flowing right. I've never seen it really good but photographic evidence reveals some fantastic days. Here the water is cold and seals are the surfer's constant companion. Above California, Oregon also has good waves but the cold is almost unbearable and a thick wetsuit is essential, even in summer.

South of Los Angeles the coastline is not so dramatic, but there are many beach breaks that do have good waves on occasions. The South Bay area has several breaks and Newport Beach can produce fair quality waves. Ex-president Nixon has a summer house next to two of the best breaks in Southern California – Cottons Point and Trestles. Swamis and La Jolla Shores near San Diego also have good waves.

EAST AND GULF COASTS: These are totally different surfing areas to the West Coast. Most waves are generated by local winds and they often lack power. In Florida the coast is very flat and surf is found at river mouths or groynes jutting out into the Atlantic. The Gulf Coast from Texas to Pensacola in Florida enjoys waves only in the aftermath of storms and hurricanes, and then only for a few hours.

Heading north from Florida there are very few spots with quality waves. New Jersey is passable on odd occasions. New York has barren beaches with coin-operated turnstiles. Long Island is a slight improvement but the waves are usually only small.

North of New York the pine forests run down onto rocky points which look capable of producing reasonable surf. A thick wetsuit and a lot of local knowledge would be essential requirements for surfing here.

MEXICO

After the USA, Mexico makes a nice change of pace, both for its culture and wave quality. Just across the border from San Diego there are quite good waves but they are rather slow-breaking. Deeper into Mexico the waves start to get hollow. Ponta Maria and Ponta Baja way down the Baja Peninsula both have strong, hollow waves.

Just to the right of Sunset is Backyard. Good from 1m to 2½m on the right swell.

CENTRAL AMERICA

Panama has some good breaks, one of them a point break similar to Rincon. And there is good surf along many areas of coastline. But access is a major problem. Also the heat and the bugs and biteys of the tropics provide a deterrent for all but the most adventurous surfers.

EQUADOR

This is an interesting country with lots of good waves and lukewarm water that provides almost no relief from the frequently stifling heat. In 1965 Mike Doyle, Bob Evans and I visited Equador after the world championships in Peru. We had good waves and enjoyed the hospitality of the local people, but the most amazing find of our trip was the abundance of balsa trees. Doyle and I carved boards from one piece of balsa wood more than one metre wide – a strange phenomenon for an Australian surfer.

PERU

Here surfing is the sport of the elite. The Club Waikiki at Mira Flores, just outside Lima, is the best equipped surf club I have ever seen. Servants wax and carry your boards to the water, and others help you dress for dinner. The waves are sloppy for most of the year but they do get big and powerful. The Humboldt Current runs down the coast so the water is very cold while the air temperature is hot.

BRAZIL

Just north of Rio there are good beach and point breaks but, as in many other South American countries, beach access is difficult.

HAWAII

From November to March Hawaii has the biggest and best surf in the world. Although all the Hawaiian islands have surf, Maui and Oahu are the most consistent. The North Shore of Oahu is the most famous surfing area in the world, home of several major international professional surfing contests.

Crowds are something of a problem on Oahu with surfing conditions often chaotic. The crowds and the ever-present racial tensions between the locals and the white 'haoles' can prove frustrating for both the novice and professional surfer, but you can still find some sanity on the garden isle of Kaui, where coral reefs produce waves all around the coastline. After the trip from the airport to Hanalei you don't even need a car. Between Hanalei Bay and the end of the road there are twenty good breaks, ranging from powerful rights at Hanalei to the easier waves of Tunnels, Cannons, and Taylors. Best time of year is December to March. Many times I've stayed on Kaui with only the barest essentials, surfing to exhaustion point and living a peaceful country existence. Maui is another island with incredible surf during the northern winter. The waves are spread around the entire island and a car is a necessity. Honolua Bay is the most famous break. It works from 2 to 4 metres and can produce the most fantastic waves in the world. It was here in 1968 that McTavish and I tested our vee-bottom boards. On 3 metres of wave face the vees held us in perfectly, and our experiments led to the acceptance of vees in modern surfboard design. There are several good breaks around the old whaling port of Lahaina, notably Maalaea, said to be the fastest right-hander in the world.

NEW ZEALAND

Here mid-summer is the best time for surfing, when the water is warmer. Surfing during winter is almost impossible and only the locals brave the freezing conditions. Most of the known good surf is on the North Island. Raglan is the most famous break, a long-running left-hand point surf on the west coast near Hamilton. It tends to close out over 3 metres but in small conditions it is a fantastic wave. Also on the west coast, Piha has a big reputation but in my opinion it is not much more than an average beach break. Further down the coast past Gisborne is the Miahia Peninsula and for my money the finest surf in New Zealand. Rolling Stones is a fast right-hand point wave, but the entire peninsula is alive with good waves.

Sunset Beach on a normal winter's day. Four metres of rising north west swell with only fifty surfers out.

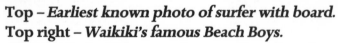

Top – *Earliest known photo of surfer with board.*

Top right – *Waikiki's famous Beach Boys.*

Above – *Duke Kahanamoku introduced surfboard riding to Australia on the 15th of January 1915 at Freshwater (now Harbord) near Manly.*

Right – *C. J. Snow McAlister Australian Champion 1926, '27 and '28.*

History through Design

ALTHOUGH we can date surfing back to before Captain James Cook's discovery of the sport of the Hawaiian kings in the eighteenth century, the development of surfing equipment is a much more recent history. Over 25 years of development have gone into the modern surfboard. The lengths have gone from 3.5 metres in 1960 down to under 2 metres in 1970 and now standardise out at around 2 metres depending on the weight and experience of the surfer. I believe we have only scratched the surface of surfboard design. In future years technology will undoubtedly play a major part in allowing the surfer even closer proximity to the deep curl of bigger waves.

The Hawaiian chiefs used 5-metre long 'olo' boards made from 'wili wili' trees. Their subjects also surfed, but on shorter 'alaia' boards carved from the koa wood of the breadfruit tree. The process of selecting a tree to build a surfboard had religious significance for the Hawaiians. Offerings were made at the base of the trunk. After felling the tree they would rough-shape it and drag it to the 'helau' or canoe shed where they would spend days carving it with stone and bone tools. Then the board would be rubbed with coral to remove the carving marks and stained with banana buds, charcoal or soot. Oil from the 'kukui' nut was then rubbed into the surface to repel water. After each use the board was rubbed with coconut oil to protect it and further repel water. The board was always kept out of the weather.

A fantastic surfer of an early era was King Kamehameha I whose prowess in the waves was still the subject of Hawaiian songs long after his death. But by the beginning of the twentieth century surfing had all but disappeared because of the doctrines preached by Christian missionaries. The missionaries claimed that surfing and many other tribal customs were profane. Surfing amongst the ordinary people ceased. The kings, however, defied the missionaries and surfed in isolation.

Duke Kahanamoku was the next great surfer to emerge. As a youth he worked as a beach boy at Waikiki and put on surfing exhibitions for the tourists, one of whom took the idea home to the American mainland. In 1908 George Freeth became the first man to ride a surfboard in the United States. The board was much like the 'alaia' in design.

Someone actually had a surfboard shipped to Australia in 1912, but it wasn't until 1915 that the sport was understood here. In that year Duke Kahanamoku visited Sydney and set a new world swimming record, 100 yards in 53.8 seconds. While here he carved a board out of a piece of sugar pine. The board was 3.6 metres long, 61 cm wide and 7.5 cm thick. Varnished it weighed 31 kg. The Duke gave an exhibition of its use at Freshwater Beach, then accessible from Sydney only by Manly ferry. Freshwater was a wide, open beach with fishermen's lean-tos scattered over it. One fisherman asked the Duke if he needed a boat ride out to the break, but the Duke declined, hopped onto his new machine and paddled out prone. The exhibition was fantastic but far too advanced for most onlookers to comprehend. Snow McAlister, who was present that day and is still a keen surfer, remembers: 'No one understood what was happening when the Duke went sideways on the wave. He started at one end of the beach and finished up at the other. We just stared in amazement. It wasn't until 1956 when the Americans showed us how to corner at Avalon that we understood what he had done. But they had fins on their boards.'

On his departure the Duke presented the board to a young Australian called Claude West. The board was later hung in the Freshwater Surf Lifesaving Club where every year since it has been lovingly revarnished by either Claude or **Snow McAlister. Claude West** went on to become the Australian boardriding champion ten years in a row. He worked for an undertaker, gained a sound knowledge of wood and began experimenting in 1932 with hollowed-out redwood planks. Around the same time an American called **Tom Blake** started building hollow boards made from redwood strips.

Perhaps because surfing was so closely tied to the lifesaving clubs in Australia, design really took a turn for the worse in the 1930s. The lifesavers were interested in paddling competitions and their boards were designed for fast paddling rather than for riding waves. They were about 6 metres long, and about 45 centimetres wide and to ride a wave straight to the beach you had to negotiate the drop, quickly turn the board sideways to slow down and not get knocked off by the wave's energy, then spin it around again in the white water, continuing to the beach. Tricks were limited but very spectacular. Snow McAlister tells the story of a contest at Newcastle when he got a beauty, a big green slide way outside. The board paddled so fast that he was able to get into a headstand as he slid down the face towards the beach, holding his breath as the wave poured over him. He held the manoeuvre until his fingertips touched the sand. An official came over and confirmed that Snow had won the Australian Championship while he was still on his head.

While Australian surfboards limited wave riding the Americans didn't advance much during that period either. They continued to design their boards like the original Hawaiian prototypes. Here, one advancement of sorts was the invention of the surf-ski. **Dr G. A. Crackenthorp** of Manly had problems handling the conventional surfcraft and built a cedar plank he could sit on. It was 2.61 metres long, 50.5 cm wide, and 15 cm thick. Its low centre of gravity made it easier to balance on, much like today's modern skis. The doctor's inventiveness has resulted in a form of surfing that is less physically taxing than board surfing.

A Californian called **Bob Simmons** is widely recognised as the father of modern surfboard design. While most Californians had copied the longer boards used by the Hawaiian kings, Simmons stuck to the concept of the commoners – shorter, wider designs. His major breakthrough came in 1948 when he shaped a board from balsa wood, covered it with fibreglass to keep out the water and stuck a fin on the tail to hold a line across a wave. Simmons recognised, as had many Hawaiians before him, that the power directions didn't lead straight into the beach. His design ideas spread like wildfire through California.

Simmons later developed another design he called the 'hot curl board', built to outrun the curl. It was a finless board for perfect days at Malibu when the tail design would hold him in that critical spot in the curl. I've surfed one of these original Simmons designs at Malibu and was truly amazed. The board wouldn't turn, but the idea of dispensing with fins is still strong today.

Mystery still surrounds Simmons' death in 1953 at Windansea Beach in California. The surf that day was neither big nor dangerous, but after Simmons entered the water he was never seen again. His board was later washed up on the beach and it was assumed he had drowned.

In 1956 **Hobie Alter** and **Dave Sweet** made the first boards shaped from plastic foam. They faced innumerable problems. The foam shrank, the moulds were hard to work with, but by the early 1960s the foam boards were beginning to replace balsa all along the Californian coast. Sweet supplied the Los Angeles surfers while Alter looked after San Diego. Soon the surfing population was estimated at 5,000, and the Beach Boys, 'Ride the Wild Surf' and Gidget burst onto the scene.

The same year that Alter and Sweet began experimenting with foam, a group of American and Hawaiian surfers visited Australia to compete in the Olympic surf carnival at Torquay. On their way home they displayed their talents at Avalon Beach, north of Sydney. They were outpaddled by the Australians on their longer, narrower boards, but the visitors' wave-riding ability was so superior that several young locals fought to purchase the boards from them.

Within months a local board industry had sprung up, with **Bill Clymer, Barry Bennett, Gordon Woods,** and **Danny Keough** going into production on Sydney's northside, and **Bill Wallace** and **Norm Casey** starting up on the southside. The new Malibu boards were between 3 and 3.3 metres long and around 60 cm wide, with rounded noses and squared off 20 cm tails. Originally they were made of plywood over a timber frame because balsa wood was unobtainable until 1958. The most popular designs, apart from the 'Malibu', which the Americans had introduced in 1956, were the 'pig' and 'teardrop' shapes (with tail lift, narrow noses, and little nose lift) and, the 'sausage' was particularly popular, with a full and rounded nose and tail, and parallel rails, and it rode well.

Phil Edwards was the next designer to make significant changes. He was a unique surfer with a huge cult following in Southern California. Around Los Angeles **Dewey Weber, Lance Carson** and **Mickey Dora** were the idols with their quick footwork, hot-dog styles. But it was the smooth and functional surfing of Edwards that influenced design concepts. And the biggest initial change was in length. Phil had an old 3.5 metre balsa board he called 'Baby', and on her he developed a surfing style that consisted of smooth flowing turns, trimming and looking cool. He went to work for Hobie Alter and as foam took over, no Californian surfer would ride anything under 3 metres. Edwards' models were 80 cm wide with three redwood strips down the centre. In Australia **Midget Farrelly** was his protege and I ran a close second in Edwards' imitation. Midget and I built hundreds of these boards until 1964 when the first World Titles at Manly brought **Joey Cabell, Mike Doyle** and **LJ Richards** to Australia. Midget had copied Phil's style to a tee, and he knew the local waves better than the Americans did. He took the title but the new thing was Cabell. Doyle and LJ were both impressive but Cabell was amazing. He used the front half of the board more than anyone else. His designs were shorter and wider, more stable and more manoeuvrable because they were lighter. Cabell had foresaken good looks and done away with the heavy redwood strips.

Sydney board-builder Greg McDonagh made the perfect Cabell imitations, and we were off on a new trip of close to the curl manoeuvring. The Australian master of the Cabell style was **Bob McTavish**. Bob was a strong and stocky little flower child who moved about the coast between Noosa and Sydney, living out of an old Ford and experimenting with his surfboards and his surfing.

George Greenough had already made one trip to Australia, and I heard stories about him from Russell Hughes and Algy Grud. They told me about this guy who would spot a school of tuna on the horizon, tear off down the coast in the direction they were headed, paddle out to sea on a ski he had fixed up and intercept the school. Many a fine evening has been spent eating George's fantastic catch around the fireplace he had built on the floor out of two old wash tubs and a piece of down pipe. The man is a genius and I've come to know him well since those early days at Noosa. Recently I was surfing at Lennox Head when up beside me popped George himself, telling tales of his seven-month adventure sailing to Australia from his home in California in a boat he built himself. A magnificent man of the sea.

Greenough's most significant contribution to surfboard design was his fin. The theory behind the Greenough fin was borrowed from the fish. He found that fibreglass fins have an ability to store energy and hold it for a time before snapping back upright. The fins he developed enabled surfers to gain acceleration coming out of turns. But George's main problem in design has been that he was and is a kneeboard rider. Many frustrating years were spent trying to apply his hull theory to surfboards without any great degree of success. I believe the reason is simply that kneeriders have a lower centre of gravity and different design principles apply to them. Nonetheless, George revolutionised fins and got the ball rolling for kneeriders.

On his 1967 trip to Australia, Greenough turned many people on to kneeriding and the advantage of allowing the surfer to fit into smaller places inside the wave to give that added sensation of complete involvement with

Top left – *The scene at San Onofre in 1939.*

Top right – *60's surf stars leave California for Endless Summer promotion trip.*

Left – *Surfers at Malibu in the late 50's.*

Above – *Midget Farrelly in perfect quasimoto at North Narrabeen.*

Above – *The author with pintail (forehand) and squaretail (backhand) designs in 1969.*

Below – *The main problem was the fins kept breaking at the base. The author mid-60's at Long Reef.*

Top right – *Victoria's most famous surfer Wayne Lynch half-way through the manoeuvre he was most acclaimed for.*

Right – *Innovative designer of surf and sail boards, Bob McTavish.*

the wave. Greenough's 'spoon' board was 1.5 metres long, 50 cm wide, and was designed as a displacement hull. He started its construction by shaping the bottom, glassing it up to the rails, and rolling it over. Then he hollowed it out from the top, leaving foam for buoyancy around the nose and rails. The back tapered to nothing to attain flex, as had been done with fins.

I won the 1966 World Titles at San Diego on a board I called 'Sam.' Sam owed a bit to Cabell designs, but more, it was a copy of the boards Bob McTavish was riding. Greenough sanded a flex fin for it. The following year McTavish and I developed a board to take to Hawaii that really broke new ground. We called it our 'Fantastic Plastic Machine'. It was 2.5 metres long, 52 cm wide, with 23 cm square tail. The new boards were pretty radical. The Californians were still riding sluggish boards and concentrating on riding the nose like **David Nuuhiwa.**

The important innovation was the V-shaped bottom. The boards had 10 cm vee in the tail which rolled into a belly under the nose. You could bank off a turn like no other board I had ridden. They trimmed well but were hard to bring off the top or cutback.

At this point in Hawaii a lot of good surfers were starting to ride a fine-lined faster design first made by **Dick Brewer.** Brewer was and is a fine craftsman but he lacked the surfing ability to test his boards through the refining stage. **George Downing,** on the other hand, was thinking along similar design lines and could test them. But the first surfer I ever saw put the new fast board theory into practice and combine it with unique manoeuvrability was Joey Cabell. The man we'd all copied a few years earlier was our inspiration again in the late 1960s, carving cleaner, faster lines than anyone I had seen.

In 1969 I spent three months in Kaui (an Hawaiian outer island) looking at Cabell's designs and watching him surf. A true surfer, he put his amazing quiver of boards through endless trials, always pushing them to the limits. I brought back one of his designs and started making them on my farm at Byron Bay. They were completely different to the current Australian boards and soon there were copies everywhere. Some were good, some bad, but overall their influence resulted in the standard surfboard design we know today.

During this period I did not see my friend, Victorian surfer **Wayne Lynch,** but it was interesting to note when we did meet again he was riding an almost identical board. In the years that followed I developed my surfing and surfboards along similar lines to Cabell's, and my boards are still based on his theories.

Surfboard design today is an accumulation of the ideas and theories of all the designers I have mentioned – surfers who thought creatively and were willing to put their ideas to the test.

The standard modern surfboards is around 2 metres long and 50 centimetres wide. The planshape or outline is either a rounded full pintail, a swallow tail, or soft square tail with varying notches or flyers off the rails near the tail. These flyers or notchers are used by a number of excellent surfers to give you a corner to bite from – they are there to make the board more responsive and get the width of the tail narrower allowing the board to ride a bigger range of surf. A narrower tail is necessary for bigger waves allowing the tail to hold in the wave face and not spin-out. The widest point is also the thickest point, usually about 10 to 20 centimetres behind half-way, with the width and thickness tapering towards the nose and tail. The rails are low in profile near the nose, softer in the middle and hard-edged in the tail. To appreciate what all that means let's look at the variables.

PLANSHAPE: This is the most obvious variable, governing both curves and dimensions. The curve should be smooth. Outline curve seems to work best when the widest point is where the surfer's front foot will be in the standing position. A common planshape mistake is an overly straight tail. This makes the board hold to a certain course, creating difficulties when a quick direction change is required.

The longer a surfboard, the longer its turning circle, so the length of a board is relevant to the size of the waves you wish to ride. Two to 2.3 metres is usually long enough for waves up to 3 metres, providing the rider is of average weight and height. For bigger waves length increases proportionately. Width at the widest point generally remains constant at around 45 to 55 centimetres. Extra width makes the board more stable but cuts down speed and hangs you up in hollow waves. Nose and tail width also remain constant at 25 to 30 centimetres, and both are critical. Too much tail area makes the board break out on turns, and too little bogs it down in the water. Flyers or tail notches were introduced to overcome this and allow narrower tails with enough area to turn without bogging down.

BOTTOM SHAPE: This has been developed extensively over the past eight years, helped along by Simmons' original theories and the experiments McTavish and I made with the vees. Vee in the tail under your back foot helps the board hold in the water. Flat bottoms accelerate faster but curved bottoms seem capable of greater speed on good-sized waves. Length curve is rather too complex to explain in a few words. Each shaper has his own preferences and in my opinion it is the design feature that can make or break a board. My bottom template is fifteen years old, developed from that original Cabell board back in 1969. Most boards these days combine vees, flats and concaves. A concave section makes the nose plane quicker, the flat section gives stability and, as I have said, vees hold in the water. Some designers are doing flutes and channels in the bottom of the board with the idea of giving more lift, making the board plane out quicker and improve acceleration.

RAILS: Not much recent development here. It has been found that a low rail, which is a rail with its profile in the bottom half, is the best for all around surfing. The most protuding part of the rail being about two-thirds of the thickness. How soft they are depends on the surfer's ability. Good surfers can handle harder, more definite rails. My own and all that I manufacture have hard edges all the way around to give definite direction in a turn. They do not bite into the wave's surface because the hard edge is tucked under the planshape, an idea I borrowed from snow skiing where hard edges are necessary for immediate direction change.

FINS: The fin hasn't changed radically since Greenough came up with his design more than twenty years ago, although there have been certain refinements. It has been found that the bigger and deeper the fin is, the more drag it creates and the harder it is to turn. Wide-based fins elongate the turning arc (suitable for big waves but not for small). Like Simmons, I have found that it is possible to surf without a fin on a well-designed board, but you must have near-perfect waves. For this reason I like my fins as small as possible, while still big enough to hold the board on course.

The further forward the fin is placed the more erratic and loose the board's response. If it is set too far forward the board will spin out on every turn. The further back it goes the stiffer the board is to turn. The surfer has to turn right on the tail. The perfect fin placement can only be found by trial and error, and this is why the movable fin box is so invaluable.

Ever since the Simmons era in the 40's, surfboards have been built with multi fins. In the early 70's we saw the re-emergence of the twin fin on small boards under 2 metres. In 1977 **Mark Richards** from Newcastle put twin fins on all his small wave boards and went on to become four times World Champion in 1979, '80, '81, '82. In 1980 nearly every surfer around the world was riding a twin fin. They were designed for more radical manoeuvres on the wave face with less importance on tube riding. It is a fact that twin fin surfboards improved manoeuvrability because your back foot is right over the fin, also the flat sides on the inside of the fins produce cavitation or lift. This makes the surfboard accelerate quicker. However a lot of surfers couldn't handle the excessive looseness, especially older surfers who were used to doing big forehand turns. Even some younger ones had problems with the twins, especially on their backhand or in bigger stronger surf.

One of these surfers was **Simon Anderson** from Narrabeen in Sydney. In 1981 Simon designed a three fin thruster with one extra fin down the middle of the twin. Tri-fins had been around since the 70's, but Simon, as well as myself were trying to tone down the excessive looseness of the twins. From '81 to the time of writing ('85) the thruster has been the most widely acclaimed board in the world. Just about every new board manufactured is a thruster with the exception of the quad or four fins, **Glen Winton** from the Central Coast started building them in 1981, after being disillusioned with both the twins and the thrusters. Apparently they ride like a twin with a bit more zest. At the annual Bells Beach contest in Victoria Mark Richards was riding a quad which asks the obvious question, What's next – five, six or ten fins?

FIBREGLASS: According to Pliny, the Roman historian, the ancient Phoenicians deserve the credit for discovering glass. He tells that the crew of a ship landed at the mouth of a river in Syria. When they were ready to cook their dinner, they could find no stones on which to support their cooking pot, so they used lumps of nitre (a sodium compound) from the ship's cargo. The heat of the fire melted the nitre, which mixed with the surrounding sand and flowed out as a stream of liquid glass.

This story may or may not be true. But some lucky accident was responsible for man's first knowledge of glass. Glass beads and charms have been found in tombs which date back as far as 7000 BC, the origin of these being either Syrian or Egyptian.

The first report of glass fibres was from seventeenth-century England where molten glass was fired on an arrow from a bow. In 1713 a Frenchman, Rene de Reaumer, submitted glass fabric woven by the Venetian Camo Riva to the Paris Academy of Science and subsequently gowns were made from this fabric. Naturally these clothes were discarded because the fabric was too coarse to be folded, not to mention the extreme irritation and discomfort that occurs when fibreglass comes in contact with the skin.

Certainly world wars played a major part in the production of fibreglass as we know it today. The Germans in World War I, while searching for a substitute to imported asbestos, produced fibreglass and resin sheets. The Americans were using fibreglass saturated with resin to manufacture aircraft parts during World War II, and it was here that the first idea of using fibreglass in surfboard construction came from. Bob Simmons worked for 'Aerospace' in Pasadena, California, a private firm which received government contracts. All information in plastics and fibreglass was classified military information but as soon as the War was over and the information declassified, Simmons made the first fibreglass board. The 283.5 g cloth was for tooling aircraft parts and the resin had no catalyst but was set off with cobalt (metal salts) driers.

The core was made of Equadorian balsa. This breakthrough allowed Simmons to make his surfboards lighter than anyone before him. After years of surfing the solid redwood and redwood and pine combination boards prior to the War, the fibreglass resin and balsa combination gave him the perfect medium to bring the boards down in size, with the first rail-shape making for 100 per cent more manoeuvrability.

Sometime in the near future someone will come up with a substitute for foam and fibreglass. There has been no change since the 1950's and we are due for one. Sophisticated moulding systems and manufacturing techniques must catch up with surfing sometime, making boards lighter, cheaper and more resistent to damage.

Opposite – Peter Townend holding the Campbell Brothers innovative design 'The Bonzer'.

Above – Newcastle's Mark Richards who took the early 70's America concept of the twin fin and redesigned both fins and board.

Top right – Michael Peterson unquestionably the finest surfer in Australia in the mid 70's.

Bottom right – Australia's Glen Winton is responsible for the latest four fin design.

Below – Cheyne Horan with his Ben Lexan designed winged keel fin.

PART 3
ALTERNATIVE SURFING

Riding a Malibu

Opposite – *The author executing a drop knee or three point turn.*

Flash of a by-gone era when the Malibu was King.

THE Malibu board totally revolutionised surfboard-riding. In 1956 a team of Californian and Hawaiian lifeguards came to Australia for the Queen's Surf Carnival held in Torquay, Victoria, in conjunction with the Olympic Games. This group brought with them the latest Malibu style surfboard. Prior to '56 all surfboards used in Australia had been the tooth-pick style which were surfed straight to the beach or at best on a slight angle away from the curl.

The name 'Malibu' came from the famous beach in California of the same name, where all the principal development had taken place in the early 50's. Their construction was of balsa wood (Australia's first were made of plywood over a timber frame) but by 1960 foam had superseded balsa all over the world.

In the late 50's Malibus varied in length from 2.5 metres to 4 metres averaging out around 3 metres. Because of the length they had excellent momentum, especially in small surf where the wave had no push. Malibus work best under these conditions and can be surfed with a fun attitude. The quality of the wave shape is not as important as on smaller modern surfboards. It is this fact that has led to the revival of the Malibu board. In

the 80's we have seen a resurgence of interest in Malibu. These modern Mals as they are called are basically the same shape as the ones of the 50's and 60's except that with the modern materials available the boards are much lighter. The length also varies considerably but most are around 3 metres. Some have tri fin set-ups and others traditional single fins. Personally I find the multi fins turn a little too easily and for that reason I use a single fin set-up. Contests have been held specifically for Malibus for the last few years with substantial prize money being offered. These contests are divided into two categories – Modern Mal, with a limit of 8' in length and Traditional Mal over 8'. Remember that a Malibu is not as refined as a modern surfboard which means that the movements of the surfer have to be more blatant. Also the leg rope is not a good idea on the old Mals because they have much more weight than the modern boards. They can do a nasty injury after a wipeout and you will have a problem getting a rope long enough to let you make a clean nose ride. However, many people do use cords with Modern Mals – it certainly puts an end to swims to the beach but it really isn't traditional Malibu surfing.

The Malibu is surfed in a manner totally different to the old toothpicks or

Backhand turn – executed correctly the weight is distributed evenly over both feet. The position on either side of the board is dependent on the degree of direction change required.

Forehand turn – turning from a trim position is difficult on a Malibu – it is much easier when made from the tail with the board out of trim.

Above – a copy-book tip stall by Neil Purchase of Byron Bay.

Left – the cheater five is the classic trim – master of the manoeuvre is Hawaii's Jeff Hakman.

modern surfboard. As well as the unique manoeuvres and tricks that can only be performed on a Malibu, there is a great amount of style that should be shown in the correct execution of these manoeuvres and tricks.

STYLE: Style in Malibu surfing or in any sport for that matter is defined as that personal ingredient that makes individual sportsmen and women stand out among their peers. The late 50's, early 60's, was a period of great development of individual styles of surfing. It can best be illustrated by comparing two very talented individuals from that period. Phil Edwards of the classic or functional style and Dewey Weber of the hot dog or radical style.

HOT-DOG: This style is the first one used on Malibus in the mid 50's. It involves constantly throwing the board around as much as possible on the wave face and doing as many tricks as you can. It is more flamboyant than the functional style and wearing big baggy brightly coloured trunks with long blonde hair was the style of early Hot-Dog surfers.

CLASSIC OR FUNCTIONAL: This style was in vogue in the early 60's and gave most attention to the poise and grace of movement. To show smooth flowing turns with ballet-like artistry was the key thought of functional surfing. The manner in which the hands were held, an inclination with the head, a nose tweek in a particularly critical part of the wave, subtlety was the key-word to the repertoire of the functional surfer.

Big flowing turns, trimming and stalling the board were the important manoeuvres of the cool, calm and collected functional surfer. Some manoeuvres like nose riding and drop knee turns were exhibited with the arms held high in the air which looked more artistic and still impresses the judges.

FOREHAND TURN: The movement is basically the same as turning a modern board except that more effort must be produced in the actual bend and push. Often it is necessary to start the walk out of the turn anticipating the next position on the wave. Turning can be executed in both the top and bottom of the wave and must be made from right on the tail of the board. When top turning it is necessary to lean back slightly on the back foot and for bottom turns leaning forward helps the flow into the next manoeuvre.

DROP KNEE OR BACKHAND TURN AND CUTBACK: This manoeuvre in itself is the singularly most important in Malibu surfing. In my opinion its correct execution shows the true artistry of the Malibu surfer making it totally unique. It is, as the name implies, a drop knee turn where the back leg is bent so the knee almost touches the deck of the board. Pres-

The Malibu is impossible to manoeuvre in the curl however many tricks can be performed in the curl en route to the shoulder.

sure is then felt evenly through both legs along the rail which is making the curve for the turn.

The action and position of the body are exactly the same as downhill turning on cross country skis. Sometimes it is necessary to stand on one side of the board and other times over the centre, depending on the next manoeuvre and the amount of drive needed from the turn.

TRIMMING: Trim is the name given to the fastest speed the surfboard is capable of. To set the board in trim the surfer usually walks forward after the turn and then inches his way either back or forward to feel for the fastest speed point. This trim position is usually two-thirds of the length of the Malibu towards the nose or just a little forward of halfway, depending on the plan shape and bottom curve.

The most dynamic trim is the cheater five or strauch crouch where the surfer gets into a low crouch on the front third of the board. The weight is then moved back onto the bent back leg, the forward leg is stretched up towards the nose – arms are held in casual style.

STALLING: This manoeuvre is used when the Mal has outrun the curl, or looks like it will in the next few seconds. The basic stall is instigated by lifting the nose high in the air off the tail but more often than not a good drop knee cut back will take you back to the curl with more style. Nose riding is the most dynamic stall manoeuvre in Malibu surfing – it takes a skilled sense of timing and a high degree of ability to get a good nose ride. The board is of the utmost importance. The better nose riders have a wide full plan shape with plenty of tail-lift. This creates the necessary drag in the tail that lets the surfer balance on the other end. At the height of the Malibu era in California in the early 60's they had whole contests devoted to nose riding. The winner sometimes rode the nose for over a minute. There are three categories of nose riding: hang five, hang ten, and the classic tip stall.

THE TIP STALL: is the classic nose ride. In most cases the rider has trimmed the board on the front third for a normal critical section and realizes that a nose ride is possible. In this position take care not to nose dive – this is a common mistake when the wave has a steep face.

HANGING FIVE: is the first step to **HANGING TEN** and usually it's a matter of the wave or section shape that decides either five or ten toes to be dribbled over the nose. Once you have got that far it doesn't take much to get five or ten toes over. Sometimes it is necessary to combine a tip stall on the front section of the board with hanging five or ten in order to keep your balance and the boards momentum. Some Mal surfers put their hands in the

Below – *The talented Mark Warren halfway through a powerhouse cutback in short board style. However this is not a traditional Malibu turn.*

Opposite – *Malibus are extremely difficult to hold in on big waves however in yesteryear waves of up to 8 metres were ridden successfully on old Malibus.*

air, others behind their backs and others don't know what they're doing because it's so much fun.

WALKING THE BOARD: This manoeuvre is extremely subtle and marks the difference between good and bad Mal surfers. The basic rule is step cleanly and precisely, foot over foot between each step. My rule is don't shuffle. It looks bad and takes more time.

KNEE PADDLING: Because of the relatively small length of modern boards all paddling has to be done lying flat on your stomach in a prone position. But the Malibu can be paddled in prone or up on your knees. It's really only a matter of finding the balance point and getting the board moving.

In order to get maximum speed from knee paddling, I found getting up on your toes and leaning as far forward as possible to strike the water gives you much more power and speed but this power position cannot be prolonged for any great length of time, due to the physical endurance required.

Because the original Malibus were too big to manoeuvre in the curl many tricks were invented as you passed through the curl on your way to the shoulder.

HEAD DIP: Usually performed off the front third of the board, the surfer bends over at the waist and sticks his head in the curl. In the functional Mal era, one of the most classic stalls was to slow the board off the tail and further slow it with a well timed head dip.

QUASIMOTO: While streaking through the curl in full trim, take a low crouch position, put one arm forward, the other back, both parallel to the wave face. Keep the head down and hold until you are out of the curl.

It is important not to hold this position outside the curl area.

EL TELEPHONO: This manoeuvre is the quasimoto with the arm closest to the curl raised and bent to the ear simulating the use of the telephone.

COFFIN RIDE: This little trick should be performed in a trim position in the curl. The surfer sits down, puts his legs straight out in front and lies down, his arms either by his sides or in symbolic prayer position.

THE HEAD STAND: After a wave has closed out the surfer bends down and adopts the normal head stand. Obviously, this is a very difficult trick. It is especially hard to keep the board moving towards the beach without wiping out.

THE SPINNER: Another popular trick of the 60's is a 360 spin which is made by the surfer as he walks the board. It is difficult to keep your balance as you are turning around but with a bit of practise it becomes quite easy.

Flippers tucked up in a driving bottom turn.

Kneeboarding

THE art of kneeboarding is similar to conventional boardriding in that a fibreglass clad, hand shaped foam board is used to ride waves. Kneelos, as kneeboard-riders are known, can be found riding all sorts of waves around Australia's coastline. The obvious difference between kneelos and conventional surfers is that kneelos do it on their knees. This important distinction in riding position gives kneeboarding its unique character and appeal.

One of the great advantages is that of having a low centre of gravity and being capable of fitting into very tight situations; parts of the wave where other surfers would have great trouble maintaining control. A slight draw-back of the kneeling position is that a heavy weighting and unweighting between the front of the board and the tail can't be achieved in the same manner as a stand up surfer does between his front and back feet.

The above characteristics mean that the shape and design of kneeboards are quite different to stand up boards. A good kneeboard must be capable of being put into a trim position and turned from the one position on the board, with only a slight weight transfer from knees to ankles being the movement to initiate this change. The low centre of gravity means that a kneeboard can be quite wide throughout and also have the fin(s) set a fair way up from the tail. This, in conjunction with a good constant rocker through the bottom, means the above can be achieved. In the days of single fins, a long raked flexible fin was often positioned up to 50 cm from the tail. The advancement of design, the desire of kneelos to surf harder, and to per-form more difficult manoeuvres has led to the introduction of kneeboards with four fins. Again these fins are set quite forward (usually at least 33 cm from the tail). The tri-fin set up also has a strong following in some areas.

When first considering to buy a board, the novice should look for one which is suited to his/her weight and height and can therefore be easily paddled. A kneeboard with a full outline and fairly simple in shape is prob-ably the best to learn on. The fact that kneeboards are shorter, usually between 160 cm-170 cm, means that extra width throughout is an advan-tage for both paddling and stability. As the ability of the surfer increases he can contemplate custom ordering certain tail shapes and other aspects of design, such as edges, flyers etc to compliment his/her style and manner of surfing.

Most kneelos wear flippers, they are not essential, but do help to push through waves when paddling out and to give extra thrust on take off. One thing, try not to kick your flippers in other surfers faces as you paddle, because it is most annoying.

As with any sport, kneeboarding does tend to exert certain pressures on the human body. With kneelos, it is their knees which can cop a hiding. The

David Parkes with a state of the art kneeboard.

113

Above – *A young Peter Crawford with his slab design kneeboard.*

Opposite – *A lower centre of gravity and being a smaller target for the curl means the Kneelo can take off deeper than the average surfer.*

simplest way to avoid this is to wear neoprene kneepads. Most wetsuit manufacturers produce them and they are well worth the small investment. Another way is to affix a padding to the deck of the board. If either of these two methods are used, the likelihood of any knee injury is probably no greater than any other sport.

Kneelos come into their own when the waves are hollow and 'sucky' The ease of getting to your knees, the instant acceleration that flippers give on take off and the soft nose entry of a good kneeboard means that late take offs deep inside are par for the course. The manner in which a kneelo surfs the wave is uniquely different to other surfriders, not better or worse, just different. The fact that kneeboards lend themselves to sitting in the tube, accounts for the fact that when a good kneelo is out in the surf he/she can usually be found looking for the power pocket by drawing smooth functional lines that are aimed at finding that elusive (or not so elusive!) tube section.

To me, the rush achieved by taking off straight into the tube, looking out the end, and then finally gliding through the opening is far more satisfying than any on the face 'trick' manoeuvre.

As far as contests go in Australia, kneelos are well catered for. The Australian Surfriders Association, which is responsible for amateur surfing, has included kneelos in the Australian Titles since 1974. Such is the high standard of Australian kneeboarding that since the first international event involving Australian kneelos in 1978 when Neil Luke and myself competed in Hawaii, until Michael Novokov's 1984 World Title win, Australia has won every event. There are a couple of kneeboard clubs in Sydney as well as one in Perth and on the Gold Coast. They provide a good opportunity to meet other kneelos and for the beginner to learn more about kneeboarding. Clubs, in conjunction with the local A.S.A. contests, provide both a social and competitive forum. Since kneeboarding is appealing to both recreational and competitive surfers and enjoys a following from all walks of life it should continue to grow and develop as the rest of surfing does.

David Parkes

115

Taking off – leaning in the direction you want to go; using the paddle to maximum advantage.

Wave Skis

WHEN Nat first asked me to put this together I thought it would be an easy task, for I have been teaching people the basics for years, but there is a vast difference in oral instruction and by the written word, but it should be done and I shall break it down as simply as possible, in everyday English.

TYPES OF WAVE SKIS

There are three types of skis in the mass production market place. First a (hollow) – moulded ski. This ski is the most common because it is the cheapest. The ski is moulded in two halves and joined together at the seam. It has a bung near the nose to allow water to drain out after each use, and is normally fitted with footstraps and an adjustable fin. The size of the ski normally ranges from 195 cm to 315 cm and priced around the $350 to $400 with a cheap paddle thrown in. The main disadvantage is they crack around the seam and leak, and do not perform as well as the others.

THE FOAM FILLED MOULDED SKI: This is similar in construction to the hollow ski, but it is injected with foam. The advantage is obvious, the foam adds strength eliminating the stress factor, and adding rigidity which gives the ski a much better performance and less dings. This ski is normally fitted with tri-fins, seat belt and paddle-rope holder. The price is around the $450-$500 mark, with a size range 180 cm to 285 cm. Some models have channels, adjustable seat belt boxes, and footwell fittings.

CUSTOM BUILT SKI: This is the Rolls Royce of Wave Skis. Hand-shaped from foam the same way as a surfboard, it is sprayed and cased in fibreglass, and has all the advantages of a surfboard. Light manoeuvrable and choice of design by the surfer himself. The only disadvantage is they ding a lot easier than the moulded variety. Basic price ranges from $600 to $700. Most competitive surfers use them.

Before we move on, there are two other types of ski's that are being sold, but in very small numbers. They are the **soft-ski** which is built from Morey Boogie foam and is much safer than the other varieties, but is expensive (around $500), and the **Camel Knee-Ski.** The Camel is a cross between a Canoe and a Ski where the rider kneels on the craft and is supported by a trunk in the centre. This ski is rotationally moulded from plastic and is priced around $400.

SELECTING A SKI

The first thing you should ask yourself is how much can I afford to spend. If you have about $300 you would be better off buying a good second hand ski rather than a cheap and nasty hollow 'no name' model. The 'no name' is probably a non functional design which has been thrown together to cash

in on the boom, where as a 'brand' name usually has a back up warranty and good track record in the market place. Your height, weight and experience are the next contributing factors. If you are average height and weight 175 cm and weigh 72 kg and used to surf before you got married, you are the average surf skier. You would be looking for a ski around 220 cm to 230 cm depending on how much time you are going to spend on it. The more water-time, the shorter the ski because 'the shorter the craft the better the performance'.

TYPES OF PADDLES

There are wooden, fibreblass, aluminium and plastic paddles. The rule of thumb is the bigger the price, the better the paddle. The size of the paddle should be approximately 25 cm longer than your body height. When selecting a paddle think of how much you want to spend. A good fibreglass paddle will set you back approximately $70, but for $45 you can pick up a reasonable brand name with aluminium shaft that will get you out there. Now, do you want an offset (one blade offset to the other) or a set of straight blades (parallel to each other)? The reason for offset blades is the blade out of the water is parallel to the water therefore cutting down wind resistance. Also when doing an Eskimo Roll it offers less resistance. The straight blades are of course easier to use. You do not have to roll the wrist and when doing the eskimo roll you can 'feel' the position of the paddle under water.

ACCESSORIES

PADDLE ROPES: These are used to attach the paddle to the ski for safety reasons. When the rider falls off he keeps hold of the paddle which is attached to the ski via the cord, preventing the ski from flying around or hitting other people in the water. It can also save you from a long swim.

SEATBELT: The seatbelt is the same belt the divers use for keeping themselves on the bottom. Nylon webbing with a stainless steel or plastic buckle attachment. The seatbelt straps the rider to the ski allowing him to roll over and right himself without getting off the ski. The quick release buckle can be undone by simply pulling the strap. Beginners should not use a seat belt until the Eskimo Roll has been perfected in still water with someone around to lend assistance, should you get stuck upside down.

HOW TO START

You have purchased your first ski, you are dying to get out in the surf and try it out. Take my advice, **don't.** Try and find some still water (a lake, swimming pool, estuary, dam, river) where there is some shallow water. Now straddle the ski like a horse, with both legs dangling over the side. When you

Sequence – the Eskimo roll is an absolute necessity for the ski rider. Beginners should not use a seat belt to practise this manoeuvre.

Opposite – Phil Avalon with a custom-made wave ski.

feel comfortable and the ski's nose is level with the water and the tail is not sinking, paddle casually. If you begin to lose your balance don't allow your torso to get rigid. Relax and rock with the imbalance, then gradually straighten the torso and begin to paddle again.

To turn around paddle, one side a couple of extra strokes and the ski will turn in the opposite direction. The amount of time spent in still water is as important as your first time in the surf, as the more competent you are, the easier it will be for you when the first wave picks you up and hurtles you towards the shore. My advice is spend sixteen hours in still water before 'hitting the surf' to build up your confidence.

GETTING OUT: There are laws of common sense, and or surf sense.
1 Check the area for current's or rips that may be dangerous.
2 Study the break and decide which way the waves are breaking. (If they are breaking to the left and there is a channel on the right, use the channel to get out.)
3 If the current is running from left to right over a sandbank look for the spot that is not being hammered by waves. The deeper water is always a clue. The current can be utilized to get out.
4 Keep away from the flagged area and other surfers (whilst learning).
5 Have someone watch you from the beach.

CATCHING A WAVE: Make sure you are perfectly steady when paddling. If you tilt to the left or right on take-off the ski will automatically veer off in that direction. When you sight an oncoming wave, determine the direction the wave is moving, and angle your ski towards the shoulder. Paddle slowly and steadily picking up speed until the wave is under you and carrying you down the face. Lean forward towards the wave to turn, drifting your paddle into the face at a 45° angle to assist the turn. When the broken wave catches up, lean back momentarily until you feel the push of the wave. Again choose which direction you wish to travel and push the paddle into the broken wave and continue the ride.

FINS

THE SINGLE BASELESS FIN: This fin was the first fin adapted by ski riders: The fin has a narrow base with a bloomp on the end. The theory is that the bloomp on the end pivots the ski around.

THE BUTTERFLY FIN: Designed by an American board rider who was looking for twin-fin performance from a single base. The result was the Butterfly. The fin gives a shorter-arc turning circle, and is very loose which is surprising from such a wide base. This fin is widely used by wave ski enthusiasts world wide and has had excellent results in competitions. The fin is unbreakable.

TRI-FIN: The Tri-Fin was first used by the writer in 1979, when twin fins were popular. I wanted to have the choice of running the ski with a twin-fin system or as a single. (I also ran it a couple of times with 3 fins but found the ski a bit stiff.) Then in 1980 Nat Young and Simon Anderson both developed tri-systems with smaller fins (or in Nat's case a larger centre fin). They also widened the area of the tail of the surfboard and Simon won the Surfabout and Bells contests on a tri-fin.

Then the Thruster was born and set the industry on fire. Ski riders took to them like wildfire, but the lower centre of gravity and different weight distribution (no front foot) caused several problems. Surfers like John Christensen soon ironed them out. The outside fins should be toed in towards the nose, with the centre fin back in a tri-angular set-up for maximum performance.

CROSS FIN: I have been experimenting with a centre fin that has an added wing through the centre, the idea was supplied by Jim Newton. The trial and error period was exhausting, but exhilarating. This fin will be used in conjunction with the two outside fins. It traps water between the base of the ski and the wing, eliminating bump and bounce in choppy conditions, holding the tail down on re-entries, assisting the rider to pull the ski out of a nose dive, and give extra bite in turns.

4 FIN: Glen Winton was responsible for the four fin. When asked by a TV commentator on how he came up with the design Glen answered "I just took one fin out"... the audience thought Glen was being funny, but he was serious, he had been using a five fin board. But since then the four fin has been refined and is part of every stand-up surfers quiver. The system is similar to a twin fin except the fins are scaled down. The twin fin's weakness was it did slide out in bigger waves, the extra fins eliminate that problem, but on a ski they tend to 'stiffen' the tail a bit too much for my liking, but a couple of manufacturers are beginning to add clinker channels for better release.

SUMMARY

The wave ski or surf ski is now at its peak, associations and clubs have now sprung up in every part of Australia, UK, France, South Africa, USA and Europe. Wave skis are a happening alternative.

Phil Avalon

Locked-in, using the boards edge and body weight to carve in the curl.

Riding a Boogie Board

NOT long after I could confidently swim a couple of lengths of the local pool right around the time I first became interested in riding waves I can recall dodging speeding surfoplanes while bodysurfing at my local beach.

In those days every metropolitan beach had surfo rentals and these inflatable rubber mats really gave you a thrill. For ten shillings you could be shooting down the face of big dumpers all day long, squealing with deilght as the foam engulfed you before gripping the handles for a bumpy laughable ride to shore.

Somehow the surfoplane craze died and in the early seventies a Californian surfboard designer named Tom Morey came up with a concept of a solid soft plastic foam board. Within a few short years the Boogie board was being used all over the world by intending surfboard riders as their first craft and a whole new direction within surfing had opened up. The only major improvement over the old surfoplane was the Boogie's potential for allowing the surfer to travel sideways across the wave in the same manner as a surfboard.

HOW TO CHOOSE THE RIGHT BOOGIE BOARD FOR YOU

The first thing to consider is your size and weight. There are a great many models on the market from the cheaper ones around $60 to the super pro model around $200.

The cheaper models are smaller and therefore have less buoyancy. They are OK for smaller kids up to 52 kgs. They are made of compact foam rubber that is extremely flexible and really it's here that the big difference comes in Boogies.

In essence what you pay for is the rigidity of the foam or the stiffness of the board. The more expensive models you can't bend at all and the cheapies are like spaghetti. The stiffer the board, the easier it is to hold an edge when angling across the face. The pro models are bigger which means they float larger people. They also have a slick running surface on the bottom sometimes of a thin plastic skin and on the more developed models a hard plastic sheet that gives better planing at slower speeds and gets the board up and going faster. When this sheet joins the rail an edge is created around the entire board. This edge is a reference point that is used when carving turns and gives the board its incredible manoeuvrability.

Some Boogies even come with fin boxes that allow normal surfboard fins to be fitted.

In my opinion the best all-round Boogie for the beginner of average weight is in the one hundred dollar range. They are around 106 cm long and 52 cm wide. They have reasonably good rigidity with a smooth skin all over the board and come with a wrist cord that has a limited life expectancy.

Most good surf shops carry a full range from the pro models to the cheapies and the salesperson should be able to run you through the range and best advise you for your weight, experience and budget.

One thing I might mention is the care that should be taken when storing Boogies – keep it away from the dog as foam seems to have an irresistible appeal. Also, take care around fires as Boogies tend to melt with intense heat and be careful not to lay them on sharp objects as this punctures the skin. Repairs are possible with contact cement but are a hassle that can be avoided with a bit of thought.

BOOGIE ACCESSORIES

FLIPPERS, OR SWIM FINS: These essential accessories come in a variety of shapes and sizes. The proven best design for Boogies are imported from California and are made by Churchill. They have a scalloped or cut away shape on the inside corner and are made of a soft flexible rubber that floats and does not irritate the foot and yet still delivers plenty of power. This scalloped shape is important if you ever intend to kneel up as the fin fits very neatly under you and you are not in fact sitting on a fin.

IN THE BUDGET LINE: The Australian made Continental flippers are of a different design that works well enough as long as you get the correct fit. Unlike the Churchill which have a strap around the heel, the Continental has a cup the shape of the heel.

They are made of a harder rubber and come in two colours. This is important because the blue ones float, the black don't. This is handy if you happen to lose one.

In order to protect your flippers from coming off, there are two alternatives; flipper grippers which are leg ropes that tie to the flipper, the other end attaching around your ankle. This design is good for the strap style flipper but keepers are better for the cup style. They consist of another cup that slips over the fin and holds on with a strap over your ankle.

Most new Boogie boards come with wrist ropes attached, basically they are a means of keeping the board within arm's length of the rider when a wave washes them off. Some boards come with quality cords, others are a bit suspect. A broken cord or velcro wrist strap can be easily replaced for around $10 and are readily available at your local surf shop. The telephone cord style Boogie cord is a sensible idea, because the coiled urethane makes the cord shorter and it does not get in the way and tangle around your hand as the traditional style cord does.

Another good idea for your Boogie is a handle. This can be easily attached

Above – *takeoff lying over the back of the board, holding onto the rail and nose, kicking to gain momentum.*
Opposite – *Rolling the board up onto a rail for the bottom turn.*

A canvas covered inflatable rubber mat is another alternative that will always put a smile on your face.

HOW TO RIDE A BOOGIE

Just like everything else a great deal can be learnt by watching other more experienced riders. Obviously you must follow all the basic rules set out in Chapter 1 (Starting Out), Chapters 4 and 5 covering going into the ocean and catching a wave.

Put on your flippers as close to the waters edge as possible, negotiate the shore break and get yourself out the back via the rip. You will find yourself in the line-up.

For your first experiences it is a good idea to stay right away from the board riders. On the edge of the flagged area is a good spot. If you are surfing in the flags don't be alarmed as Boogies are permitted in this area because of the soft material used in manufacture but generally board riders are in the better waves either surfing left or right which is also the best place for you to surf.

On a Boogie you' can get a lot closer to the shore than board riders because the Boogie does not have the buoyancy and momentum to get up and catch the wave as quickly as a board.

This means you will have to learn to negotiate more critical take-offs but because of the shorter length the difference between full nose dive and perfect trim is only a few centimetres. The actual catching of the wave varies, sometimes if the wave is very full and hard to catch it will be necessary to lay completely off the back of the board, kicking as hard and deep as possible to get the board to plane as fast as possible. Other times on more critical take-offs, a small kick and you will be on it. It should not be necessary to paddle as your legs and flippers should deliver plenty of power. If you paddle you have to let go of the board and it can slip out from under you. Remember to kick nice and deep with every stroke. After a couple of foamies straight to the beach take the plunge and venture out the back for an unbroken wave. Once on the wave pull the board in under you and lay on one side, leaning to either the left or right depending on the direction the curl peels. You will find the board responds and angles in the direction your body weight dictates so movement on the wave face is a matter of leaning in the direction and keeping the board planing. More complex manoeuvres like spins where the board rotates 360° on the wave face and barrel rides where the surfer gets so far back in the tube the board can be rolled up the face and pulled over with the breaking curl are moves that come with experience and persistence. It's a lot easier for a Boogie rider to get in the tube as they are a smaller target for the breaking curl but still the rider will be well advised to keep his eyes open in the tube to avoid the breaking curl by ducking his head and moving his body weight to trim through the curl.

to the front of the board by screwing the board with a screw driver. It comes in handy for holding the board under waves while duck-diving and puts a lot less strain on the wrist rope.

Fins that can be attached to the bottom of the board along each side are another useful accessory. They are attached in the same manner as a handle and come in a kit with a template to trace the position on the board. They are particularly helpful when learning to turn and for first going sideways across the wave.

A lot of novices have problems staying on the wave face without slipping sideways. Fins really are of assistance and as a general rule they should be fitted as close to the rail as possible.

Glossary

Nose Riding – *Surfing manoeuvre where the surfer stands on the very front of the surfboard.*

Action Traction:	Non slip substitute for wax
Aggro:	Agression in the water
Animal:	Aggressive approach to surfing
Arc:	Line of turn on a wave
A.S.A.:	Australian Surfriders Association
A.S.P.:	Association of Surfing Professionals
Backhand:	Term for surfing with your back to the wave
Bank:	Sandbank
Barrel:	Tube (see Tube)
Beachbreak:	Surf breaking on a sandbank close to beach
Blown Out:	Choppy conditions caused by strong or onshore wind
Bombora:	Deep water reef well off shore
Boogie Board:	Soft foam board surfed in prone position
Bottom turn:	Turn out of bottom of wave
Carve:	To surf excellently (ie "he was carving")
Catalyst or Hardener:	Chemical ingredient used for mixing with resin to make it harden
Channel:	1. Gap between sandbanks or reefs 2. Design feature on bottom of board
Clean:	Good glassy surf conditions
Clean up:	Big set of waves that washes surfers into beach
Close out:	A situation where waves break simultaneously along the entire length of a beach
Concave:	Design feature on bottom of board to give extra lift
Cornering:	Going sideways across a wave

Curl:	A part of a hollow or semi-hollow wave that loops over as it breaks
Curve:	Design feature (ie curve in bottom of board)
Cutback:	The surfing manoeuvre used to change direction and head back towards the breaking part of the wave
Deck:	The top surface of a surfboard
Ding:	Damage to surfboard
Drive:	Acceleration on wave
Drop:	The initial part of the ride where you head to the base of the wave
Drop in:	To take off on a wave when rider is already surfing
Duck Dive:	Method of diving the board under an oncoming wave on the way out through the break
Dumper:	The type of wave that sucks out in shallow water and pounds when breaking
Edge:	Design feature on board (see rail)
Eskimo roll:	Method of going under waves for Malibus and wave skis
Face:	Unbroken surface of a wave
Fall Line:	The line of fastest descent to the base of a wave (or mountain slope)
Fibreglass:	Woven glass cloth that, when saturated with resin, provides the protective outer coating of a surfboard
Fin or Fins:	Small vertical projections on the rear of the bottom of the surfboard used for stability and drive
Fins or Flippers:	Swimming aid worn on feet
Flat:	1. Surfless ocean 2. Powerless section of wave
Flick off:	A manoeuvre used to kick the board clear of the breaking wave
Foam:	Polyurethane plastic material used to make the core of the surfboard
Forehand:	Where the surfer stands facing the wave
Glassy:	Smooth ocean surface conditions when there is no wind
Goofy Foot:	A surfer who rides with his right foot in front of his left
Grommet:	Cheeky young surfer
Ground Swell:	Swell which has travelled a long distance from where it has formed; characterised by evenness and length
Gun:	Large surfboard for riding big waves

Hollow:	Descriptive term denoting cylindrical type of wave
Hot:	Slang term for a good quality wave
Huey:	Legendary God of Surf
Impact Zone:	The point at which the breaking wave lands and exerts maximum force
Indicator:	Reef or sandbank seawards of surf spot that shows when a set of waves is approaching
Inside:	1. In the tube 2. Closest to curl on take-off 3. Shoreward of breaking wave
Kneeboard:	A surfboard, usually shorter, ridden on the knees
Kneelo:	Kneeboard rider
Layback:	Manoeuvre of the 80's where the surfer is surfing on his backhand and lays out on his back on the wave face.
Left (hander):	A wave breaking from left to right when viewed from shore
Leg-Rope	A rubberised or urethane cord used to attach the surfboard to the rider's ankle
Line-Up:	The term used to describe the wave and swell formation at a surfing location
Lined-Up:	Descriptive term indicating long even swells
Lip:	The pitching edge of a HOLLOW or semi-hollow wave
Logger:	Old Malibu
Malibu:	1. Length 8'6" to 10'6" style of surfboard from the 50's and 60's originally made of Balsa (plywood in Australia) and eventually foam and fibreglass. 2. A beach in Southern California
Natural or Natural Foot:	A surfer who rides with his left foot in front of his right
Nose:	The front of the surfboard
Nose Riding:	Surfing manoeuvre where the surfer stands on the very front of the surfboard
Off the lip:	Manoeuvre involving striking the breaking lip of the wave
Offshore:	Conditions when the wind is blowing off the land
Onshore:	Conditions when the wind is blowing onto the land
Outside or out the Back:	A position beyond the line of breaking waves
Peak:	A wave whose maximum height is attained over only a very small area, sloping away to either side … produced by triangular reef or sandbank

Pearling:	Where the nose of the surfboard goes underwater – usually on take-off
Pintail:	Design feature on tail section of board
Plan shape:	Outline of surfboard
Pocket:	Part of wave under breaking lip
Pointbreak:	Surfbreak where waves peel alongside a point
Prone-out:	Process involving heading for shore and going from standing to lying position on board
Pullout:	A surfing manoeuvre where the rider gets off the wave
Radical:	Outrageous style of surfing
Rail:	The side or edges of a surfboard
Reef:	A submerged area of rock causing waves to break
Re-entry: (Floater)	Surfing manoeuvre where the surfer heads up into, and comes over with, the breaking part of the wave
Resin:	Chemical substance used to saturate fibre-glass
Right:	A wave breaking from right to left when viewed from shore
Rip:	Concentrated local current usually running out to sea where water brought in by breaking waves escapes to the open sea
Rocker:	The curve of lift in a surfboard shape when viewed from side
Rocket Block:	Hard foam block that attaches to the back of the thruster style board to give position of back foot
Roundhouse:	Cutback that takes the surfer through 180 degrees
Roundtail:	Design feature on tail section of board
Sandbank:	A submerged area of sand causing waves to break
Session:	A period of time spent surfing
Set:	A group of waves following one after another
Shorebreak:	A surf breaking close to the beach
Shoulder:	The part of the wave close to the curl that has not yet broken
Spinner:	360 degree turn by surfer on Malibu Board
Spin-out:	When the board breaks out of the wave face
Spring suit:	Wetsuit with either long or short arms and short legs
Squaretail:	Design feature on tail section of board
Stall:	Surfing manoeuvre where the board is slowed up for the curl to catch up
Steamer:	Full wetsuit with long arms and legs
Stringer:	Thin piece of timber glued down the middle of the foam core to give lateral strength
Sucky:	An extremely hollow style of wave
Surf ski:	A piece of surfing equipment ridden while sitting down and propelled by paddle
Surfo-plane:	Inflatable rubber mat used on Australian beaches in the 50's
Swallowtail:	Design feature on tail of surfboard
Swell:	A movement through water generated by storms Waves before they break
Tail:	The back section of a surfboard
Take-off:	The first part of a ride after catching a wave
Three Sixty:	Modern manoeuvre where the surfer continues the bottom turn up through the lip. The fins then break loose and the board and surfer continue around the 360 loop on the same wave
Thruster:	Modern three fin board
Toothpick:	Australian surfboard from the 40's and 50's usually 16' long by 15" wide used primarily as racing board with limited wave riding use. Construction was plywood with a light timber frame
Top turn:	Simple turn at top of wave
Trimming:	Maximum constant speed position on a particular wave. Most relevant to riding a Malibu
Tube:	The inside of a hollow wave
Tube suit:	Wetsuit featuring short legs and no arms
Twin fin:	Two fin board
Vee:	Design feature on bottom of board
Wall:	The face or unbroken surface of a wave
Wax:	Mixture of parrifin, beeswax, incense and colouring that is rubbed on the deck of boards to aid traction
Wax Comb:	Plastic scraper with serated edge that is used to rough up old wax coat
Wedge:	Heavy, peaking wave
White water:	The breaking part of the wave after it was closed out or the curl has broken
Windswell:	Swell caused by local wind conditions
Wing:	Design feature on rail of board
Wipe-out:	Where the surfer gets hit by the breaking wave causing him or her to fall off